COMPANION WORKBOOK

for

The Only Beginner Freeze-Drying Book You'll Ever Need

---

300 Batch Logs, Maintenance Sheets, Checklists, Reminders, Conversions & Rehydration Tips for a Freeze-Dryer Size

MEDIUM

MICRO-HOMESTEADING EDUCATION

GO.2MHE.COM

This Workbook belongs to:

_____

TABLE OF CONTENTS

Information Worksheets

Quick Start Worksheets

Kitchen Worksheets

Foods You Cannot Freeze-Dry

Foods You Can Freeze-Dry

Other Record Keeping

Join Our Community

IMPORTANT INFORMATION
ABOUT MY FREEZE-DRYER

Chosen Name [   ]

Size Option [   ]

Model Number [   ]

Serial Number [   ]

Purchase Date [   ]

Order Number [   ]

Software [   ]

Updates [   ]

Vacuum Pump [   ]

Oil Change Info [   ]

Preferred Oil [   ]

Customer Service [   ]

HOME FREEZE-DRYER INFORMATION

Specifications		Small	Medium	Large	X-Large
Current Price	Color Stainless Steel	$2,495 $2,695	$3,195 $3,395	$3,895 $4,095	$5,295
Size	Width Depth Height	17.4" W x 21.5" D x 26.8" H	19" W x 25" D x 29" H	21.3" W x 27.5" D x 31.3" H	24.3" W x 37.4" D x 35.6" H
FD Weight		61 lbs SS 80 lbs	112 lbs SS 133 lbs	138 lbs SS 161 lbs	265 lbs
Premier Vacuum Pump Weight		32 lbs	32 lbs	32 lbs	35 lbs
Shipping Weight		139 lbs SS 150 lbs	212 lbs SS 221 lbs	253 lbs SS 274 lbs	370 lbs
Average Power Draw		9-10 amps/hr. Spikes to 16.	10-11 amps/hr. Spikes to 16.	10-12 amps/hr. Spikes to 16.	12-14 amps/hr. Spikes to 16.
Power Needs		110 Volt Outlet. Dedicated 20 amp circuit recommended. No GFCI.		110 Volt Outlet NEMA 5-20. Dedicated 20 amp circuit REQUIRED. No GFCI.	

Food Information		Small	Medium	Large	X-Large
Number of Trays		3	4	5	6
Tray Size	Width Length Height	7.75" W x 14" L x 0.75" H	7.5" W x 18" L x 0.75" H	9" W x 20.5" L x 0.75" H	10.9" W x 29.5" L x 0.75" H
Max Fresh per Tray	Fluid Cups Fluid Ounces Liters Pounds Kilograms	3.3 c 27 oz 0.8 L 2.3 lbs 1 kg	4.2 c 34 oz 1 L 2.5 lbs 1.1 kg	5.9 c 47 oz 1.4 L 3.2 lbs 1.5 kg	10.5 c 83.6 oz 2.5 L 5.8 lbs 2.6 kg
Max Fresh per Batch	Fluid Cups Fluid Ounces Liters Pounds Kilograms	10 c 81 oz 2.4 L 7 lbs 3 kg	16.8 c 136 oz 4 L 10 lbs 4.5 kg	29.5 c 235 oz 7 L 16 lbs 7.5 kg	62.4 c 501.6 oz 15 L 35 lbs 15.6 kg
Max Annual Batches		200+	200+	200+	200+
Ave Pounds		4-7 lbs	7-10 lbs	12-16 lbs	25-35 lbs
Max Annual Fresh		1,400 lbs	2,000 lbs	3,200 lbs	7,000 lbs

CAPACITY

X-Large *PRO* Freeze-Dryer

Dimensions	Color: 258 lbs 24.3" W x 37.4" D x 35.6" H
Trays	7 Trays: 10.9" W x 29.5" D x 0.75" H
Max Fresh Food per Tray	10.5 cups, 83.6 oz, 2.5 L, 7.1 lbs, 3.2 kg
Max Fresh Food per Batch	72.8 cups, 585.2 oz, 17.5 L, 50 lbs, 22.4 kg
Max Annual Batches	200 batches @ 50 lbs = 10,000 lbs fresh

X-Large Home Freeze-Dryer

Dimensions	Color: 265 lbs 24.3" W x 37.4" D x 35.6" H
Trays	6 Trays: 10.9" W x 29.5" D x 0.75" H
Max Fresh Food per Tray	10.5 cups, 83.6 oz, 2.5 L, 5.8 lbs, 2.6 kg
Max Fresh Food per Batch	62.4 cups, 501.6 oz, 15 L, 35 lbs, 15.6 kg
Max Annual Batches	200 batches @ 35 lbs = 7,000 lbs fresh

Large *PRO* Freeze-Dryer

Dimensions	Color: 143 lbs, Stainless Steel: 150 lbs 21.3" W x 27.5" D x 31.3" H
Trays	6 Trays: 9" W x 20.5" D x 0.75" H
Max Fresh Food per Tray	5.9 cups, 47 oz, 1.4 L, 4.2 lbs, 1.9 kg
Max Fresh Food per Batch	35.4 cups, 282 oz, 8.4 L, 25 lbs, 11.4 kg
Max Annual Batches	200 batches @ 25 lbs = 5,000 lbs fresh

Large Home Freeze-Dryer

Dimensions	Color: 138 lbs, Stainless Steel: 161 lbs 21.3" W x 27.5" D x 31.3" H
Trays	5 Trays: 9" W x 20.5" D x 0.75" H
Max Fresh Food per Tray	5.9 cups, 47 oz, 1.4 L, 4.2 lbs, 1.9 kg
Max Fresh Food per Batch	29.5 cups, 235 oz, 7 L, 16 lbs, 7.5 kg
Max Annual Batches	200 batches @ 16 lbs = 3,200 lbs fresh

CAPACITY

Medium *PRO* Freeze-Dryer

Dimensions	Color: 119 lbs, Stainless Steel: 127 lbs 19" W x 25" D x 29" H
Trays	5 Trays: 7.5" W x 18" D x 0.75" H
Max Fresh Food per Tray	4.2 cups, 34 oz, 1 L, 3 lbs, 1.4 kg
Max Fresh Food per Batch	21 cups, 170 oz, 5 L, 15 lbs, 7 kg
Max Annual Batches	200 batches @ 15 lbs = 3,000 lbs fresh

Medium Home Freeze-Dryer

Dimensions	Color: 112 lbs, Stainless Steel: 133 lbs 19" W x 25" D x 29" H
Trays	4 Trays: 7.5" W x 18" D x 0.75" H
Max Fresh Food per Tray	4.2 cups, 34 oz, 1 L, 2.5 lbs, 1.1 kg
Max Fresh Food per Batch	16.8 cups, 136 oz, 4 L, 10 lbs, 4.4 kg
Max Annual Batches	200 batches @ 10 lbs = 2,000 lbs fresh

Small *PRO* Freeze-Dryer

Dimensions	Color: 91 lbs, Stainless Steel: 98 lbs 17.4" W x 21.5" D x 26.8" H
Trays	4 Trays: 7.75" W x 14" D x 0.75" H
Max Fresh Food per Tray	3.3 cups, 27 oz, 0.8 L, 2.3 lbs, 1 kg
Max Fresh Food per Batch	13.2 cups, 108 oz, 3.2 L, 9 lbs, 4 kg
Max Annual Batches	200 batches @ 9 lbs = 1,800 lbs fresh

Small Home Freeze-Dryer

Dimensions	Color: 61 lbs, Stainless Steel: 80 lbs 17.4" W x 21.5" D x 26.8" H
Trays	3 Trays: 7.75" W x 14" D x 0.75" H
Max Fresh Food per Tray	3.3 cups, 27 oz, 0.8 L, 2.3 lbs, 1 kg
Max Fresh Food per Batch	10 cups, 81 oz, 2.4 L, 7 lbs, 3 kg
Max Annual Batches	200 batches @ 7 lbs = 1,400 lbs fresh

Keep track of how the foods process in your freeze-dryer.

Batch #		Start Cooling	Trays In	Trays Out	Run Time	Extra Dry	Total
		am pm	am pm	am pm	hrs	hrs	hrs
Start Date:		Customize Temp	Time	Check Time:	am pm	am pm	am pm
End Date:		Freeze					Subtract Dry from Wet for Water Loss
		Dry		mTorr:			
Tray Contents Description:	Examples: Raw, Cooked, Thickness, Liquid, Spread	Pre-Frozen	Wet grams	Check 1 grams	Check 2 grams	Dry grams	
1		Y / N					
2		Y / N					
3		Y / N					
4		Y / N					
Notes			Chamber Cleaned: Y / N	Oil Changed: Y / N	Maint. Needed: Y / N		

Batch #		Start Cooling	Trays In	Trays Out	Run Time	Extra Dry	Total
		am pm	am pm	am pm	hrs	hrs	hrs
Start Date:		Customize Temp	Time	Check Time:	am pm	am pm	am pm
End Date:		Freeze					Subtract Dry from Wet for Water Loss
		Dry		mTorr:			
Tray Contents Description:	Examples: Raw, Cooked, Thickness, Liquid, Spread	Pre-Frozen	Wet grams	Check 1 grams	Check 2 grams	Dry grams	
1		Y / N					
2		Y / N					
3		Y / N					
4		Y / N					
Notes			Chamber Cleaned: Y / N	Oil Changed: Y / N	Maint. Needed: Y / N		

Batch #		Start Cooling	Trays In	Trays Out	Run Time	Extra Dry	Total
		am pm	am pm	am pm	hrs	hrs	hrs
Start Date:		Customize Temp	Time	Check Time:	am pm	am pm	am pm
End Date:		Freeze					Subtract Dry from Wet for Water Loss
		Dry		mTorr:			
Tray Contents Description:	Examples: Raw, Cooked, Thickness, Liquid, Spread	Pre-Frozen	Wet grams	Check 1 grams	Check 2 grams	Dry grams	
1		Y / N					
2		Y / N					
3		Y / N					
4		Y / N					
Notes			Chamber Cleaned: Y / N	Oil Changed: Y / N	Maint. Needed: Y / N		

Keep track of how the foods process in your freeze-dryer.

Batch #		Start Cooling	Trays In	Trays Out	Run Time	Extra Dry	Total
		am pm	am pm	am pm	hrs	hrs	hrs
Start Date:		Customize Temp	Time	Check Time:	am pm	am pm	am pm	
End Date:		Freeze						Subtract Dry from Wet for Water Loss
		Dry		mTorr:				
Tray Contents Description:	Examples: Raw, Cooked, Thickness, Liquid, Spread		Pre-Frozen	Wet grams	Check 1 grams	Check 2 grams	Dry grams	
1			Y / N					
2			Y / N					
3			Y / N					
4			Y / N					
Notes				Chamber Cleaned: Y / N	Oil Changed: Y / N	Maint. Needed: Y / N	

Batch #		Start Cooling	Trays In	Trays Out	Run Time	Extra Dry	Total
		am pm	am pm	am pm	hrs	hrs	hrs
Start Date:		Customize Temp	Time	Check Time:	am pm	am pm	am pm	
End Date:		Freeze						Subtract Dry from Wet for Water Loss
		Dry		mTorr:				
Tray Contents Description:	Examples: Raw, Cooked, Thickness, Liquid, Spread		Pre-Frozen	Wet grams	Check 1 grams	Check 2 grams	Dry grams	
1			Y / N					
2			Y / N					
3			Y / N					
4			Y / N					
Notes				Chamber Cleaned: Y / N	Oil Changed: Y / N	Maint. Needed: Y / N	

Batch #		Start Cooling	Trays In	Trays Out	Run Time	Extra Dry	Total
		am pm	am pm	am pm	hrs	hrs	hrs
Start Date:		Customize Temp	Time	Check Time:	am pm	am pm	am pm	
End Date:		Freeze						Subtract Dry from Wet for Water Loss
		Dry		mTorr:				
Tray Contents Description:	Examples: Raw, Cooked, Thickness, Liquid, Spread		Pre-Frozen	Wet grams	Check 1 grams	Check 2 grams	Dry grams	
1			Y / N					
2			Y / N					
3			Y / N					
4			Y / N					
Notes				Chamber Cleaned: Y / N	Oil Changed: Y / N	Maint. Needed: Y / N	

M FREEZE-DRYER BATCH LOGS PAGE#

Keep track of how the foods process in your freeze-dryer.

Batch #		Start Cooling	Trays In	Trays Out	Run Time	Extra Dry	Total
		am pm	am pm	am pm	hrs	hrs	hrs
Start Date:		Customize Temp	Time	Check Time:	am pm	am pm	am pm
End Date:		Freeze					Subtract Dry from Wet for Water Loss
		Dry		mTorr:			
Tray Contents Description:	Examples: Raw, Cooked, Thickness, Liquid, Spread	Pre-Frozen	Wet grams	Check 1 grams	Check 2 grams	Dry grams	
1		Y / N					
2		Y / N					
3		Y / N					
4		Y / N					
Notes			Chamber Cleaned: Y / N	Oil Changed: Y / N	Maint. Needed: Y / N		

Batch #		Start Cooling	Trays In	Trays Out	Run Time	Extra Dry	Total
		am pm	am pm	am pm	hrs	hrs	hrs
Start Date:		Customize Temp	Time	Check Time:	am pm	am pm	am pm
End Date:		Freeze					Subtract Dry from Wet for Water Loss
		Dry		mTorr:			
Tray Contents Description:	Examples: Raw, Cooked, Thickness, Liquid, Spread	Pre-Frozen	Wet grams	Check 1 grams	Check 2 grams	Dry grams	
1		Y / N					
2		Y / N					
3		Y / N					
4		Y / N					
Notes			Chamber Cleaned: Y / N	Oil Changed: Y / N	Maint. Needed: Y / N		

Batch #		Start Cooling	Trays In	Trays Out	Run Time	Extra Dry	Total
		am pm	am pm	am pm	hrs	hrs	hrs
Start Date:		Customize Temp	Time	Check Time:	am pm	am pm	am pm
End Date:		Freeze					Subtract Dry from Wet for Water Loss
		Dry		mTorr:			
Tray Contents Description:	Examples: Raw, Cooked, Thickness, Liquid, Spread	Pre-Frozen	Wet grams	Check 1 grams	Check 2 grams	Dry grams	
1		Y / N					
2		Y / N					
3		Y / N					
4		Y / N					
Notes			Chamber Cleaned: Y / N	Oil Changed: Y / N	Maint. Needed: Y / N		

Keep track of how the foods process in your freeze-dryer.

Batch #		Start Cooling	Trays In	Trays Out	Run Time	Extra Dry	Total
		am pm	am pm	am pm	hrs	hrs	hrs
Start Date:		Customize Temp	Time	Check Time:	am pm	am pm	am pm
End Date:		Freeze					
		Dry		mTorr:			Subtract Dry from Wet for Water Loss
Tray Contents Description:	Examples: Raw, Cooked, Thickness, Liquid, Spread		Pre-Frozen	Wet grams	Check 1 grams	Check 2 grams	Dry grams	
1			Y / N					
2			Y / N					
3			Y / N					
4			Y / N					
Notes				Chamber Cleaned: Y / N	Oil Changed: Y / N	Maint. Needed: Y / N	

Batch #		Start Cooling	Trays In	Trays Out	Run Time	Extra Dry	Total
		am pm	am pm	am pm	hrs	hrs	hrs
Start Date:		Customize Temp	Time	Check Time:	am pm	am pm	am pm
End Date:		Freeze					
		Dry		mTorr:			Subtract Dry from Wet for Water Loss
Tray Contents Description:	Examples: Raw, Cooked, Thickness, Liquid, Spread		Pre-Frozen	Wet grams	Check 1 grams	Check 2 grams	Dry grams	
1			Y / N					
2			Y / N					
3			Y / N					
4			Y / N					
Notes				Chamber Cleaned: Y / N	Oil Changed: Y / N	Maint. Needed: Y / N	

Batch #		Start Cooling	Trays In	Trays Out	Run Time	Extra Dry	Total
		am pm	am pm	am pm	hrs	hrs	hrs
Start Date:		Customize Temp	Time	Check Time:	am pm	am pm	am pm
End Date:		Freeze					
		Dry		mTorr:			Subtract Dry from Wet for Water Loss
Tray Contents Description:	Examples: Raw, Cooked, Thickness, Liquid, Spread		Pre-Frozen	Wet grams	Check 1 grams	Check 2 grams	Dry grams	
1			Y / N					
2			Y / N					
3			Y / N					
4			Y / N					
Notes				Chamber Cleaned: Y / N	Oil Changed: Y / N	Maint. Needed: Y / N	

M   FREEZE-DRYER BATCH LOGS

Keep track of how the foods process in your freeze-dryer.

Batch #		Start Cooling	Trays In	Trays Out	Run Time	Extra Dry	Total
		am pm	am pm	am pm	hrs	hrs	hrs
Start Date:		Customize	Temp	Time	Check Time:	am pm	am pm	am pm	
End Date:		Freeze							Subtract Dry from Wet for Water Loss
		Dry			mTorr:				
Tray Contents Description:	Examples: Raw, Cooked, Thickness, Liquid, Spread		Pre-Frozen	Wet grams	Check 1 grams	Check 2 grams	Dry grams	
1			Y / N					
2			Y / N					
3			Y / N					
4			Y / N					
Notes				Chamber Cleaned: Y / N	Oil Changed: Y / N	Maint. Needed: Y / N	

Batch #		Start Cooling	Trays In	Trays Out	Run Time	Extra Dry	Total
		am pm	am pm	am pm	hrs	hrs	hrs
Start Date:		Customize	Temp	Time	Check Time:	am pm	am pm	am pm	
End Date:		Freeze							Subtract Dry from Wet for Water Loss
		Dry			mTorr:				
Tray Contents Description:	Examples: Raw, Cooked, Thickness, Liquid, Spread		Pre-Frozen	Wet grams	Check 1 grams	Check 2 grams	Dry grams	
1			Y / N					
2			Y / N					
3			Y / N					
4			Y / N					
Notes				Chamber Cleaned: Y / N	Oil Changed: Y / N	Maint. Needed: Y / N	

Batch #		Start Cooling	Trays In	Trays Out	Run Time	Extra Dry	Total
		am pm	am pm	am pm	hrs	hrs	hrs
Start Date:		Customize	Temp	Time	Check Time:	am pm	am pm	am pm	
End Date:		Freeze							Subtract Dry from Wet for Water Loss
		Dry			mTorr:				
Tray Contents Description:	Examples: Raw, Cooked, Thickness, Liquid, Spread		Pre-Frozen	Wet grams	Check 1 grams	Check 2 grams	Dry grams	
1			Y / N					
2			Y / N					
3			Y / N					
4			Y / N					
Notes				Chamber Cleaned: Y / N	Oil Changed: Y / N	Maint. Needed: Y / N	

Keep track of how the foods process in your freeze-dryer.

Batch #		Start Cooling	Trays In	Trays Out	Run Time	Extra Dry	Total
		am pm	am pm	am pm	hrs	hrs	hrs
Start Date:		Customize Temp	Time	Check Time:	am pm	am pm	am pm
End Date:		Freeze Dry		mTorr:			Subtract Dry from Wet for Water Loss
Tray Contents Description:	Examples: Raw, Cooked, Thickness, Liquid, Spread	Pre-Frozen	Wet grams	Check 1 grams	Check 2 grams	Dry grams	
1		Y / N					
2		Y / N					
3		Y / N					
4		Y / N					
Notes			Chamber Cleaned: Y / N	Oil Changed: Y / N	Maint. Needed: Y / N		

Batch #		Start Cooling	Trays In	Trays Out	Run Time	Extra Dry	Total
		am pm	am pm	am pm	hrs	hrs	hrs
Start Date:		Customize Temp	Time	Check Time:	am pm	am pm	am pm
End Date:		Freeze Dry		mTorr:			Subtract Dry from Wet for Water Loss
Tray Contents Description:	Examples: Raw, Cooked, Thickness, Liquid, Spread	Pre-Frozen	Wet grams	Check 1 grams	Check 2 grams	Dry grams	
1		Y / N					
2		Y / N					
3		Y / N					
4		Y / N					
Notes			Chamber Cleaned: Y / N	Oil Changed: Y / N	Maint. Needed: Y / N		

Batch #		Start Cooling	Trays In	Trays Out	Run Time	Extra Dry	Total
		am pm	am pm	am pm	hrs	hrs	hrs
Start Date:		Customize Temp	Time	Check Time:	am pm	am pm	am pm
End Date:		Freeze Dry		mTorr:			Subtract Dry from Wet for Water Loss
Tray Contents Description:	Examples: Raw, Cooked, Thickness, Liquid, Spread	Pre-Frozen	Wet grams	Check 1 grams	Check 2 grams	Dry grams	
1		Y / N					
2		Y / N					
3		Y / N					
4		Y / N					
Notes			Chamber Cleaned: Y / N	Oil Changed: Y / N	Maint. Needed: Y / N		

M   FREEZE-DRYER BATCH LOGS

Keep track of how the foods process in your freeze-dryer.

Batch #		Start Cooling	Trays In	Trays Out	Run Time	Extra Dry	Total
		am pm	am pm	am pm	hrs	hrs	hrs
Start Date:		Customize	Temp	Time	Check Time:	am pm	am pm	am pm	
End Date:		Freeze							Subtract Dry from Wet for Water Loss
		Dry			mTorr:				
Tray Contents Description:	Examples: Raw, Cooked, Thickness, Liquid, Spread		Pre-Frozen	Wet grams	Check 1 grams	Check 2 grams	Dry grams	
1			Y / N					
2			Y / N					
3			Y / N					
4			Y / N					
Notes			Chamber Cleaned: Y / N	Oil Changed: Y / N	Maint. Needed: Y / N		

Batch #		Start Cooling	Trays In	Trays Out	Run Time	Extra Dry	Total
		am pm	am pm	am pm	hrs	hrs	hrs
Start Date:		Customize	Temp	Time	Check Time:	am pm	am pm	am pm	
End Date:		Freeze							Subtract Dry from Wet for Water Loss
		Dry			mTorr:				
Tray Contents Description:	Examples: Raw, Cooked, Thickness, Liquid, Spread		Pre-Frozen	Wet grams	Check 1 grams	Check 2 grams	Dry grams	
1			Y / N					
2			Y / N					
3			Y / N					
4			Y / N					
Notes			Chamber Cleaned: Y / N	Oil Changed: Y / N	Maint. Needed: Y / N		

Batch #		Start Cooling	Trays In	Trays Out	Run Time	Extra Dry	Total
		am pm	am pm	am pm	hrs	hrs	hrs
Start Date:		Customize	Temp	Time	Check Time:	am pm	am pm	am pm	
End Date:		Freeze							Subtract Dry from Wet for Water Loss
		Dry			mTorr:				
Tray Contents Description:	Examples: Raw, Cooked, Thickness, Liquid, Spread		Pre-Frozen	Wet grams	Check 1 grams	Check 2 grams	Dry grams	
1			Y / N					
2			Y / N					
3			Y / N					
4			Y / N					
Notes			Chamber Cleaned: Y / N	Oil Changed: Y / N	Maint. Needed: Y / N		

M   FREEZE-DRYER BATCH LOGS

Keep track of how the foods process in your freeze-dryer.

Batch #		Start Cooling	Trays In	Trays Out	Run Time	Extra Dry	Total
		am / pm	am / pm	am / pm	hrs	hrs	hrs
Start Date:		Customize	Temp	Time	Check Time:	am / pm	am / pm	am / pm	
End Date:		Freeze							Subtract Dry from Wet for Water Loss
		Dry			mTorr:				
Tray Contents Description:	Examples: Raw, Cooked, Thickness, Liquid, Spread		Pre-Frozen	Wet grams	Check 1 grams	Check 2 grams	Dry grams	
1			Y / N					
2			Y / N					
3			Y / N					
4			Y / N					
Notes				Chamber Cleaned: Y / N	Oil Changed: Y / N	Maint. Needed: Y / N		

Batch #		Start Cooling	Trays In	Trays Out	Run Time	Extra Dry	Total
		am / pm	am / pm	am / pm	hrs	hrs	hrs
Start Date:		Customize	Temp	Time	Check Time:	am / pm	am / pm	am / pm	
End Date:		Freeze							Subtract Dry from Wet for Water Loss
		Dry			mTorr:				
Tray Contents Description:	Examples: Raw, Cooked, Thickness, Liquid, Spread		Pre-Frozen	Wet grams	Check 1 grams	Check 2 grams	Dry grams	
1			Y / N					
2			Y / N					
3			Y / N					
4			Y / N					
Notes				Chamber Cleaned: Y / N	Oil Changed: Y / N	Maint. Needed: Y / N		

Batch #		Start Cooling	Trays In	Trays Out	Run Time	Extra Dry	Total
		am / pm	am / pm	am / pm	hrs	hrs	hrs
Start Date:		Customize	Temp	Time	Check Time:	am / pm	am / pm	am / pm	
End Date:		Freeze							Subtract Dry from Wet for Water Loss
		Dry			mTorr:				
Tray Contents Description:	Examples: Raw, Cooked, Thickness, Liquid, Spread		Pre-Frozen	Wet grams	Check 1 grams	Check 2 grams	Dry grams	
1			Y / N					
2			Y / N					
3			Y / N					
4			Y / N					
Notes				Chamber Cleaned: Y / N	Oil Changed: Y / N	Maint. Needed: Y / N		

M FREEZE-DRYER BATCH LOGS   PAGE#

Keep track of how the foods process in your freeze-dryer.

Batch #		Start Cooling	Trays In	Trays Out	Run Time	Extra Dry	Total
		am pm	am pm	am pm	hrs	hrs	hrs
Start Date:		Customize Temp	Time	Check Time:	am pm	am pm	am pm
End Date:		Freeze					Subtract Dry from Wet for Water Loss
		Dry		mTorr:			
Tray Contents Description:	Examples: Raw, Cooked, Thickness, Liquid, Spread	Pre-Frozen	Wet grams	Check 1 grams	Check 2 grams	Dry grams	
1		Y / N					
2		Y / N					
3		Y / N					
4		Y / N					
Notes			Chamber Cleaned: Y / N	Oil Changed: Y / N	Maint. Needed: Y / N		

Batch #		Start Cooling	Trays In	Trays Out	Run Time	Extra Dry	Total
		am pm	am pm	am pm	hrs	hrs	hrs
Start Date:		Customize Temp	Time	Check Time:	am pm	am pm	am pm
End Date:		Freeze					Subtract Dry from Wet for Water Loss
		Dry		mTorr:			
Tray Contents Description:	Examples: Raw, Cooked, Thickness, Liquid, Spread	Pre-Frozen	Wet grams	Check 1 grams	Check 2 grams	Dry grams	
1		Y / N					
2		Y / N					
3		Y / N					
4		Y / N					
Notes			Chamber Cleaned: Y / N	Oil Changed: Y / N	Maint. Needed: Y / N		

Batch #		Start Cooling	Trays In	Trays Out	Run Time	Extra Dry	Total
		am pm	am pm	am pm	hrs	hrs	hrs
Start Date:		Customize Temp	Time	Check Time:	am pm	am pm	am pm
End Date:		Freeze					Subtract Dry from Wet for Water Loss
		Dry		mTorr:			
Tray Contents Description:	Examples: Raw, Cooked, Thickness, Liquid, Spread	Pre-Frozen	Wet grams	Check 1 grams	Check 2 grams	Dry grams	
1		Y / N					
2		Y / N					
3		Y / N					
4		Y / N					
Notes			Chamber Cleaned: Y / N	Oil Changed: Y / N	Maint. Needed: Y / N		

M FREEZE-DRYER BATCH LOGS PAGE#

Keep track of how the foods process in your freeze-dryer.

Block 1

Batch #		Start Cooling	Trays In	Trays Out	Run Time	Extra Dry	Total
		am pm	am pm	am pm	hrs	hrs	hrs
Start Date:		Customize Temp	Time	Check Time:	am pm	am pm	am pm
End Date:		Freeze / Dry		mTorr:			Subtract Dry from Wet for Water Loss

Tray Contents Description:	Examples: Raw, Cooked, Thickness, Liquid, Spread	Pre-Frozen	Wet grams	Check 1 grams	Check 2 grams	Dry grams	
1		Y / N					
2		Y / N					
3		Y / N					
4		Y / N					

Notes | Chamber Cleaned: Y / N | Oil Changed: Y / N | Maint. Needed: Y / N

Block 2

Batch #		Start Cooling	Trays In	Trays Out	Run Time	Extra Dry	Total
		am pm	am pm	am pm	hrs	hrs	hrs
Start Date:		Customize Temp	Time	Check Time:	am pm	am pm	am pm
End Date:		Freeze / Dry		mTorr:			Subtract Dry from Wet for Water Loss

Tray Contents Description:	Examples: Raw, Cooked, Thickness, Liquid, Spread	Pre-Frozen	Wet grams	Check 1 grams	Check 2 grams	Dry grams	
1		Y / N					
2		Y / N					
3		Y / N					
4		Y / N					

Notes | Chamber Cleaned: Y / N | Oil Changed: Y / N | Maint. Needed: Y / N

Block 3

Batch #		Start Cooling	Trays In	Trays Out	Run Time	Extra Dry	Total
		am pm	am pm	am pm	hrs	hrs	hrs
Start Date:		Customize Temp	Time	Check Time:	am pm	am pm	am pm
End Date:		Freeze / Dry		mTorr:			Subtract Dry from Wet for Water Loss

Tray Contents Description:	Examples: Raw, Cooked, Thickness, Liquid, Spread	Pre-Frozen	Wet grams	Check 1 grams	Check 2 grams	Dry grams	
1		Y / N					
2		Y / N					
3		Y / N					
4		Y / N					

Notes | Chamber Cleaned: Y / N | Oil Changed: Y / N | Maint. Needed: Y / N

M FREEZE-DRYER BATCH LOGS

Keep track of how the foods process in your freeze-dryer.

Batch #		Start Cooling	Trays In	Trays Out	Run Time	Extra Dry	Total
		am pm	am pm	am pm	hrs	hrs	hrs
Start Date:		Customize	Temp	Time	Check Time:	am pm	am pm	am pm	
End Date:		Freeze							Subtract Dry from Wet for Water Loss
		Dry			mTorr:				
Tray Contents Description:	Examples: Raw, Cooked, Thickness, Liquid, Spread	Pre-Frozen	Wet grams	Check 1 grams	Check 2 grams	Dry grams	
1		Y / N					
2		Y / N					
3		Y / N					
4		Y / N					
Notes		Chamber Cleaned: Y / N	Oil Changed: Y / N	Maint. Needed: Y / N	

Batch #		Start Cooling	Trays In	Trays Out	Run Time	Extra Dry	Total
		am pm	am pm	am pm	hrs	hrs	hrs
Start Date:		Customize	Temp	Time	Check Time:	am pm	am pm	am pm	
End Date:		Freeze							Subtract Dry from Wet for Water Loss
		Dry			mTorr:				
Tray Contents Description:	Examples: Raw, Cooked, Thickness, Liquid, Spread	Pre-Frozen	Wet grams	Check 1 grams	Check 2 grams	Dry grams	
1		Y / N					
2		Y / N					
3		Y / N					
4		Y / N					
Notes		Chamber Cleaned: Y / N	Oil Changed: Y / N	Maint. Needed: Y / N	

Batch #		Start Cooling	Trays In	Trays Out	Run Time	Extra Dry	Total
		am pm	am pm	am pm	hrs	hrs	hrs
Start Date:		Customize	Temp	Time	Check Time:	am pm	am pm	am pm	
End Date:		Freeze							Subtract Dry from Wet for Water Loss
		Dry			mTorr:				
Tray Contents Description:	Examples: Raw, Cooked, Thickness, Liquid, Spread	Pre-Frozen	Wet grams	Check 1 grams	Check 2 grams	Dry grams	
1		Y / N					
2		Y / N					
3		Y / N					
4		Y / N					
Notes		Chamber Cleaned: Y / N	Oil Changed: Y / N	Maint. Needed: Y / N	

Keep track of how the foods process in your freeze-dryer.

Batch #		Start Cooling	Trays In	Trays Out	Run Time	Extra Dry	Total	
		am pm	am pm	am pm	hrs	hrs	hrs	
Start Date:		Customize Temp	Time	Check Time:	am pm	am pm	am pm	Subtract Dry from Wet for Water Loss
End Date:		Freeze Dry		mTorr:				
Tray Contents Description:	Examples: Raw, Cooked, Thickness, Liquid, Spread		Pre-Frozen	Wet grams	Check 1 grams	Check 2 grams	Dry grams	
1			Y / N					
2			Y / N					
3			Y / N					
4			Y / N					
Notes				Chamber Cleaned: Y / N	Oil Changed: Y / N	Maint. Needed: Y / N		

Batch #		Start Cooling	Trays In	Trays Out	Run Time	Extra Dry	Total	
		am pm	am pm	am pm	hrs	hrs	hrs	
Start Date:		Customize Temp	Time	Check Time:	am pm	am pm	am pm	Subtract Dry from Wet for Water Loss
End Date:		Freeze Dry		mTorr:				
Tray Contents Description:	Examples: Raw, Cooked, Thickness, Liquid, Spread		Pre-Frozen	Wet grams	Check 1 grams	Check 2 grams	Dry grams	
1			Y / N					
2			Y / N					
3			Y / N					
4			Y / N					
Notes				Chamber Cleaned: Y / N	Oil Changed: Y / N	Maint. Needed: Y / N		

Batch #		Start Cooling	Trays In	Trays Out	Run Time	Extra Dry	Total	
		am pm	am pm	am pm	hrs	hrs	hrs	
Start Date:		Customize Temp	Time	Check Time:	am pm	am pm	am pm	Subtract Dry from Wet for Water Loss
End Date:		Freeze Dry		mTorr:				
Tray Contents Description:	Examples: Raw, Cooked, Thickness, Liquid, Spread		Pre-Frozen	Wet grams	Check 1 grams	Check 2 grams	Dry grams	
1			Y / N					
2			Y / N					
3			Y / N					
4			Y / N					
Notes				Chamber Cleaned: Y / N	Oil Changed: Y / N	Maint. Needed: Y / N		

Keep track of how the foods process in your freeze-dryer.

Batch #		Start Cooling	Trays In	Trays Out	Run Time	Extra Dry	Total
		am pm	am pm	am pm	hrs	hrs	hrs
Start Date:		Customize Temp	Time	Check Time:	am pm	am pm	am pm
End Date:		Freeze					Subtract Dry from Wet for Water Loss
		Dry		mTorr:			
Tray Contents Description:	Examples: Raw, Cooked, Thickness, Liquid, Spread	Pre-Frozen	Wet grams	Check 1 grams	Check 2 grams	Dry grams	
1		Y / N					
2		Y / N					
3		Y / N					
4		Y / N					
Notes			Chamber Cleaned: Y / N	Oil Changed: Y / N	Maint. Needed: Y / N		

Batch #		Start Cooling	Trays In	Trays Out	Run Time	Extra Dry	Total
		am pm	am pm	am pm	hrs	hrs	hrs
Start Date:		Customize Temp	Time	Check Time:	am pm	am pm	am pm
End Date:		Freeze					Subtract Dry from Wet for Water Loss
		Dry		mTorr:			
Tray Contents Description:	Examples: Raw, Cooked, Thickness, Liquid, Spread	Pre-Frozen	Wet grams	Check 1 grams	Check 2 grams	Dry grams	
1		Y / N					
2		Y / N					
3		Y / N					
4		Y / N					
Notes			Chamber Cleaned: Y / N	Oil Changed: Y / N	Maint. Needed: Y / N		

Batch #		Start Cooling	Trays In	Trays Out	Run Time	Extra Dry	Total
		am pm	am pm	am pm	hrs	hrs	hrs
Start Date:		Customize Temp	Time	Check Time:	am pm	am pm	am pm
End Date:		Freeze					Subtract Dry from Wet for Water Loss
		Dry		mTorr:			
Tray Contents Description:	Examples: Raw, Cooked, Thickness, Liquid, Spread	Pre-Frozen	Wet grams	Check 1 grams	Check 2 grams	Dry grams	
1		Y / N					
2		Y / N					
3		Y / N					
4		Y / N					
Notes			Chamber Cleaned: Y / N	Oil Changed: Y / N	Maint. Needed: Y / N		

M   FREEZE-DRYER BATCH LOGS

Keep track of how the foods process in your freeze-dryer.

Batch #		Start Cooling	Trays In	Trays Out	Run Time	Extra Dry	Total
		am pm	am pm	am pm	hrs	hrs	hrs
Start Date:		Customize Temp	Time	Check Time:	am pm	am pm	am pm
End Date:		Freeze Dry		mTorr:			Subtract Dry from Wet for Water Loss
Tray Contents Description:	Examples: Raw, Cooked, Thickness, Liquid, Spread	Pre-Frozen	Wet grams	Check 1 grams	Check 2 grams	Dry grams	
1		Y / N					
2		Y / N					
3		Y / N					
4		Y / N					
Notes			Chamber Cleaned: Y / N	Oil Changed: Y / N	Maint. Needed: Y / N		

Batch #		Start Cooling	Trays In	Trays Out	Run Time	Extra Dry	Total
		am pm	am pm	am pm	hrs	hrs	hrs
Start Date:		Customize Temp	Time	Check Time:	am pm	am pm	am pm
End Date:		Freeze Dry		mTorr:			Subtract Dry from Wet for Water Loss
Tray Contents Description:	Examples: Raw, Cooked, Thickness, Liquid, Spread	Pre-Frozen	Wet grams	Check 1 grams	Check 2 grams	Dry grams	
1		Y / N					
2		Y / N					
3		Y / N					
4		Y / N					
Notes			Chamber Cleaned: Y / N	Oil Changed: Y / N	Maint. Needed: Y / N		

Batch #		Start Cooling	Trays In	Trays Out	Run Time	Extra Dry	Total
		am pm	am pm	am pm	hrs	hrs	hrs
Start Date:		Customize Temp	Time	Check Time:	am pm	am pm	am pm
End Date:		Freeze Dry		mTorr:			Subtract Dry from Wet for Water Loss
Tray Contents Description:	Examples: Raw, Cooked, Thickness, Liquid, Spread	Pre-Frozen	Wet grams	Check 1 grams	Check 2 grams	Dry grams	
1		Y / N					
2		Y / N					
3		Y / N					
4		Y / N					
Notes			Chamber Cleaned: Y / N	Oil Changed: Y / N	Maint. Needed: Y / N		

M   FREEZE-DRYER BATCH LOGS   PAGE#

Keep track of how the foods process in your freeze-dryer.

Batch #		Start Cooling	Trays In	Trays Out	Run Time	Extra Dry	Total
		am pm	am pm	am pm	hrs	hrs	hrs
Start Date:		Customize	Temp	Time	Check Time:	am pm	am pm	am pm	
End Date:		Freeze							Subtract Dry from Wet for Water Loss
		Dry			mTorr:				
Tray Contents Description:	Examples: Raw, Cooked, Thickness, Liquid, Spread		Pre-Frozen	Wet grams	Check 1 grams	Check 2 grams	Dry grams	
1			Y / N					
2			Y / N					
3			Y / N					
4			Y / N					
Notes			Chamber Cleaned: Y / N	Oil Changed: Y / N	Maint. Needed: Y / N		

Batch #		Start Cooling	Trays In	Trays Out	Run Time	Extra Dry	Total
		am pm	am pm	am pm	hrs	hrs	hrs
Start Date:		Customize	Temp	Time	Check Time:	am pm	am pm	am pm	
End Date:		Freeze							Subtract Dry from Wet for Water Loss
		Dry			mTorr:				
Tray Contents Description:	Examples: Raw, Cooked, Thickness, Liquid, Spread		Pre-Frozen	Wet grams	Check 1 grams	Check 2 grams	Dry grams	
1			Y / N					
2			Y / N					
3			Y / N					
4			Y / N					
Notes			Chamber Cleaned: Y / N	Oil Changed: Y / N	Maint. Needed: Y / N		

Batch #		Start Cooling	Trays In	Trays Out	Run Time	Extra Dry	Total
		am pm	am pm	am pm	hrs	hrs	hrs
Start Date:		Customize	Temp	Time	Check Time:	am pm	am pm	am pm	
End Date:		Freeze							Subtract Dry from Wet for Water Loss
		Dry			mTorr:				
Tray Contents Description:	Examples: Raw, Cooked, Thickness, Liquid, Spread		Pre-Frozen	Wet grams	Check 1 grams	Check 2 grams	Dry grams	
1			Y / N					
2			Y / N					
3			Y / N					
4			Y / N					
Notes			Chamber Cleaned: Y / N	Oil Changed: Y / N	Maint. Needed: Y / N		

M FREEZE-DRYER BATCH LOGS PAGE#

Keep track of how the foods process in your freeze-dryer.

Batch 1

Batch #		Start Cooling	Trays In	Trays Out	Run Time	Extra Dry	Total
		am pm	am pm	am pm	hrs	hrs	hrs
Start Date:		Customize Temp	Time	Check Time:	am pm	am pm	am pm
End Date:		Freeze / Dry		mTorr:			Subtract Dry from Wet for Water Loss

Tray Contents Description:	Examples: Raw, Cooked, Thickness, Liquid, Spread	Pre-Frozen	Wet grams	Check 1 grams	Check 2 grams	Dry grams	
1		Y / N					
2		Y / N					
3		Y / N					
4		Y / N					

Notes | Chamber Cleaned: Y/N | Oil Changed: Y/N | Maint. Needed: Y/N

Batch 2

Batch #		Start Cooling	Trays In	Trays Out	Run Time	Extra Dry	Total
		am pm	am pm	am pm	hrs	hrs	hrs
Start Date:		Customize Temp	Time	Check Time:	am pm	am pm	am pm
End Date:		Freeze / Dry		mTorr:			Subtract Dry from Wet for Water Loss

Tray Contents Description:	Examples: Raw, Cooked, Thickness, Liquid, Spread	Pre-Frozen	Wet grams	Check 1 grams	Check 2 grams	Dry grams	
1		Y / N					
2		Y / N					
3		Y / N					
4		Y / N					

Notes | Chamber Cleaned: Y/N | Oil Changed: Y/N | Maint. Needed: Y/N

Batch 3

Batch #		Start Cooling	Trays In	Trays Out	Run Time	Extra Dry	Total
		am pm	am pm	am pm	hrs	hrs	hrs
Start Date:		Customize Temp	Time	Check Time:	am pm	am pm	am pm
End Date:		Freeze / Dry		mTorr:			Subtract Dry from Wet for Water Loss

Tray Contents Description:	Examples: Raw, Cooked, Thickness, Liquid, Spread	Pre-Frozen	Wet grams	Check 1 grams	Check 2 grams	Dry grams	
1		Y / N					
2		Y / N					
3		Y / N					
4		Y / N					

Notes | Chamber Cleaned: Y/N | Oil Changed: Y/N | Maint. Needed: Y/N

M   FREEZE-DRYER BATCH LOGS   PAGE#

Keep track of how the foods process in your freeze-dryer.

Batch #		Start Cooling	Trays In	Trays Out	Run Time	Extra Dry	Total
		am pm	am pm	am pm	hrs	hrs	hrs
Start Date:		Customize	Temp	Time	Check Time:	am pm	am pm	am pm	
End Date:		Freeze							Subtract Dry from Wet for Water Loss
		Dry			mTorr:				
Tray Contents Description:	Examples: Raw, Cooked, Thickness, Liquid, Spread	Pre-Frozen	Wet grams	Check 1 grams	Check 2 grams	Dry grams	
1		Y / N					
2		Y / N					
3		Y / N					
4		Y / N					
Notes		Chamber Cleaned: Y / N	Oil Changed: Y / N	Maint. Needed: Y / N

Batch #		Start Cooling	Trays In	Trays Out	Run Time	Extra Dry	Total
		am pm	am pm	am pm	hrs	hrs	hrs
Start Date:		Customize	Temp	Time	Check Time:	am pm	am pm	am pm	
End Date:		Freeze							Subtract Dry from Wet for Water Loss
		Dry			mTorr:				
Tray Contents Description:	Examples: Raw, Cooked, Thickness, Liquid, Spread	Pre-Frozen	Wet grams	Check 1 grams	Check 2 grams	Dry grams	
1		Y / N					
2		Y / N					
3		Y / N					
4		Y / N					
Notes		Chamber Cleaned: Y / N	Oil Changed: Y / N	Maint. Needed: Y / N

Batch #		Start Cooling	Trays In	Trays Out	Run Time	Extra Dry	Total
		am pm	am pm	am pm	hrs	hrs	hrs
Start Date:		Customize	Temp	Time	Check Time:	am pm	am pm	am pm	
End Date:		Freeze							Subtract Dry from Wet for Water Loss
		Dry			mTorr:				
Tray Contents Description:	Examples: Raw, Cooked, Thickness, Liquid, Spread	Pre-Frozen	Wet grams	Check 1 grams	Check 2 grams	Dry grams	
1		Y / N					
2		Y / N					
3		Y / N					
4		Y / N					
Notes		Chamber Cleaned: Y / N	Oil Changed: Y / N	Maint. Needed: Y / N

24

M   FREEZE-DRYER BATCH LOGS   PAGE#

Keep track of how the foods process in your freeze-dryer.

Batch #		Start Cooling	Trays In	Trays Out	Run Time	Extra Dry	Total
		am pm	am pm	am pm	hrs	hrs	hrs
Start Date:		Customize	Temp	Time	Check Time:	am pm	am pm	am pm	
End Date:		Freeze							Subtract Dry from Wet for Water Loss
		Dry			mTorr:				
Tray Contents Description:	Examples: Raw, Cooked, Thickness, Liquid, Spread		Pre-Frozen	Wet grams	Check 1 grams	Check 2 grams	Dry grams	
1			Y / N					
2			Y / N					
3			Y / N					
4			Y / N					
Notes				Chamber Cleaned: Y / N	Oil Changed: Y / N	Maint. Needed: Y / N	

Batch #		Start Cooling	Trays In	Trays Out	Run Time	Extra Dry	Total
		am pm	am pm	am pm	hrs	hrs	hrs
Start Date:		Customize	Temp	Time	Check Time:	am pm	am pm	am pm	
End Date:		Freeze							Subtract Dry from Wet for Water Loss
		Dry			mTorr:				
Tray Contents Description:	Examples: Raw, Cooked, Thickness, Liquid, Spread		Pre-Frozen	Wet grams	Check 1 grams	Check 2 grams	Dry grams	
1			Y / N					
2			Y / N					
3			Y / N					
4			Y / N					
Notes				Chamber Cleaned: Y / N	Oil Changed: Y / N	Maint. Needed: Y / N	

Batch #		Start Cooling	Trays In	Trays Out	Run Time	Extra Dry	Total
		am pm	am pm	am pm	hrs	hrs	hrs
Start Date:		Customize	Temp	Time	Check Time:	am pm	am pm	am pm	
End Date:		Freeze							Subtract Dry from Wet for Water Loss
		Dry			mTorr:				
Tray Contents Description:	Examples: Raw, Cooked, Thickness, Liquid, Spread		Pre-Frozen	Wet grams	Check 1 grams	Check 2 grams	Dry grams	
1			Y / N					
2			Y / N					
3			Y / N					
4			Y / N					
Notes				Chamber Cleaned: Y / N	Oil Changed: Y / N	Maint. Needed: Y / N	

M   FREEZE-DRYER BATCH LOGS

Keep track of how the foods process in your freeze-dryer.

Batch #		Start Cooling	Trays In	Trays Out	Run Time	Extra Dry	Total
		am pm	am pm	am pm	hrs	hrs	hrs
Start Date:		Customize Temp Time		Check Time:	am pm	am pm	am pm
End Date:		Freeze					Subtract Dry from Wet for Water Loss
		Dry		mTorr:			
Tray Contents Description:	Examples: Raw, Cooked, Thickness, Liquid, Spread		Pre-Frozen	Wet grams	Check 1 grams	Check 2 grams	Dry grams
1			Y / N				
2			Y / N				
3			Y / N				
4			Y / N				
Notes				Chamber Cleaned: Y / N	Oil Changed: Y / N	Maint. Needed: Y / N	

Batch #		Start Cooling	Trays In	Trays Out	Run Time	Extra Dry	Total
		am pm	am pm	am pm	hrs	hrs	hrs
Start Date:		Customize Temp Time		Check Time:	am pm	am pm	am pm
End Date:		Freeze					Subtract Dry from Wet for Water Loss
		Dry		mTorr:			
Tray Contents Description:	Examples: Raw, Cooked, Thickness, Liquid, Spread		Pre-Frozen	Wet grams	Check 1 grams	Check 2 grams	Dry grams
1			Y / N				
2			Y / N				
3			Y / N				
4			Y / N				
Notes				Chamber Cleaned: Y / N	Oil Changed: Y / N	Maint. Needed: Y / N	

Batch #		Start Cooling	Trays In	Trays Out	Run Time	Extra Dry	Total
		am pm	am pm	am pm	hrs	hrs	hrs
Start Date:		Customize Temp Time		Check Time:	am pm	am pm	am pm
End Date:		Freeze					Subtract Dry from Wet for Water Loss
		Dry		mTorr:			
Tray Contents Description:	Examples: Raw, Cooked, Thickness, Liquid, Spread		Pre-Frozen	Wet grams	Check 1 grams	Check 2 grams	Dry grams
1			Y / N				
2			Y / N				
3			Y / N				
4			Y / N				
Notes				Chamber Cleaned: Y / N	Oil Changed: Y / N	Maint. Needed: Y / N	

M   FREEZE-DRYER BATCH LOGS

Keep track of how the foods process in your freeze-dryer.

Batch #		Start Cooling	Trays In	Trays Out	Run Time	Extra Dry	Total
		am pm	am pm	am pm	hrs	hrs	hrs
Start Date:		Customize	Temp	Time	Check Time:	am pm	am pm	am pm
End Date:		Freeze Dry			mTorr:			Subtract Dry from Wet for Water Loss
Tray Contents Description:	Examples: Raw, Cooked, Thickness, Liquid, Spread		Pre-Frozen	Wet grams	Check 1 grams	Check 2 grams	Dry grams
1			Y / N				
2			Y / N				
3			Y / N				
4			Y / N				
Notes				Chamber Cleaned: Y / N	Oil Changed: Y / N	Maint. Needed: Y / N	

Batch #		Start Cooling	Trays In	Trays Out	Run Time	Extra Dry	Total
		am pm	am pm	am pm	hrs	hrs	hrs
Start Date:		Customize	Temp	Time	Check Time:	am pm	am pm	am pm
End Date:		Freeze Dry			mTorr:			Subtract Dry from Wet for Water Loss
Tray Contents Description:	Examples: Raw, Cooked, Thickness, Liquid, Spread		Pre-Frozen	Wet grams	Check 1 grams	Check 2 grams	Dry grams
1			Y / N				
2			Y / N				
3			Y / N				
4			Y / N				
Notes				Chamber Cleaned: Y / N	Oil Changed: Y / N	Maint. Needed: Y / N	

Batch #		Start Cooling	Trays In	Trays Out	Run Time	Extra Dry	Total
		am pm	am pm	am pm	hrs	hrs	hrs
Start Date:		Customize	Temp	Time	Check Time:	am pm	am pm	am pm
End Date:		Freeze Dry			mTorr:			Subtract Dry from Wet for Water Loss
Tray Contents Description:	Examples: Raw, Cooked, Thickness, Liquid, Spread		Pre-Frozen	Wet grams	Check 1 grams	Check 2 grams	Dry grams
1			Y / N				
2			Y / N				
3			Y / N				
4			Y / N				
Notes				Chamber Cleaned: Y / N	Oil Changed: Y / N	Maint. Needed: Y / N	

M FREEZE-DRYER BATCH LOGS

Keep track of how the foods process in your freeze-dryer.

Batch #		Start Cooling	Trays In	Trays Out	Run Time	Extra Dry	Total
		am pm	am pm	am pm	hrs	hrs	hrs
Start Date:		Customize Temp	Time	Check Time:	am pm	am pm	am pm
End Date:		Freeze					Subtract Dry from Wet for Water Loss
		Dry		mTorr:			
Tray Contents Description:	Examples: Raw, Cooked, Thickness, Liquid, Spread		Pre-Frozen	Wet grams	Check 1 grams	Check 2 grams	Dry grams	
1			Y / N					
2			Y / N					
3			Y / N					
4			Y / N					
Notes				Chamber Cleaned: Y / N	Oil Changed: Y / N	Maint. Needed: Y / N	

Batch #		Start Cooling	Trays In	Trays Out	Run Time	Extra Dry	Total
		am pm	am pm	am pm	hrs	hrs	hrs
Start Date:		Customize Temp	Time	Check Time:	am pm	am pm	am pm
End Date:		Freeze					Subtract Dry from Wet for Water Loss
		Dry		mTorr:			
Tray Contents Description:	Examples: Raw, Cooked, Thickness, Liquid, Spread		Pre-Frozen	Wet grams	Check 1 grams	Check 2 grams	Dry grams	
1			Y / N					
2			Y / N					
3			Y / N					
4			Y / N					
Notes				Chamber Cleaned: Y / N	Oil Changed: Y / N	Maint. Needed: Y / N	

Batch #		Start Cooling	Trays In	Trays Out	Run Time	Extra Dry	Total
		am pm	am pm	am pm	hrs	hrs	hrs
Start Date:		Customize Temp	Time	Check Time:	am pm	am pm	am pm
End Date:		Freeze					Subtract Dry from Wet for Water Loss
		Dry		mTorr:			
Tray Contents Description:	Examples: Raw, Cooked, Thickness, Liquid, Spread		Pre-Frozen	Wet grams	Check 1 grams	Check 2 grams	Dry grams	
1			Y / N					
2			Y / N					
3			Y / N					
4			Y / N					
Notes				Chamber Cleaned: Y / N	Oil Changed: Y / N	Maint. Needed: Y / N	

M   FREEZE-DRYER BATCH LOGS

Keep track of how the foods process in your freeze-dryer.

Batch #		Start Cooling	Trays In	Trays Out	Run Time	Extra Dry	Total
		am pm	am pm	am pm	hrs	hrs	hrs
Start Date:		Customize Temp Time		Check Time:	am pm	am pm	am pm
End Date:		Freeze					Subtract Dry from Wet for Water Loss
		Dry		mTorr:			
Tray Contents Description:	Examples: Raw, Cooked, Thickness, Liquid, Spread		Pre-Frozen	Wet grams	Check 1 grams	Check 2 grams	Dry grams
1			Y / N				
2			Y / N				
3			Y / N				
4			Y / N				
Notes				Chamber Cleaned: Y / N	Oil Changed: Y / N	Maint. Needed: Y / N	

Batch #		Start Cooling	Trays In	Trays Out	Run Time	Extra Dry	Total
		am pm	am pm	am pm	hrs	hrs	hrs
Start Date:		Customize Temp Time		Check Time:	am pm	am pm	am pm
End Date:		Freeze					Subtract Dry from Wet for Water Loss
		Dry		mTorr:			
Tray Contents Description:	Examples: Raw, Cooked, Thickness, Liquid, Spread		Pre-Frozen	Wet grams	Check 1 grams	Check 2 grams	Dry grams
1			Y / N				
2			Y / N				
3			Y / N				
4			Y / N				
Notes				Chamber Cleaned: Y / N	Oil Changed: Y / N	Maint. Needed: Y / N	

Batch #		Start Cooling	Trays In	Trays Out	Run Time	Extra Dry	Total
		am pm	am pm	am pm	hrs	hrs	hrs
Start Date:		Customize Temp Time		Check Time:	am pm	am pm	am pm
End Date:		Freeze					Subtract Dry from Wet for Water Loss
		Dry		mTorr:			
Tray Contents Description:	Examples: Raw, Cooked, Thickness, Liquid, Spread		Pre-Frozen	Wet grams	Check 1 grams	Check 2 grams	Dry grams
1			Y / N				
2			Y / N				
3			Y / N				
4			Y / N				
Notes				Chamber Cleaned: Y / N	Oil Changed: Y / N	Maint. Needed: Y / N	

M   FREEZE-DRYER BATCH LOGS

Keep track of how the foods process in your freeze-dryer.

Batch #		Start Cooling	Trays In	Trays Out	Run Time	Extra Dry	Total
		am pm	am pm	am pm	hrs	hrs	hrs
Start Date:		Customize Temp	Time	Check Time:	am pm	am pm	am pm
End Date:		Freeze Dry		mTorr:			Subtract Dry from Wet for Water Loss
Tray Contents Description:	Examples: Raw, Cooked, Thickness, Liquid, Spread	Pre-Frozen	Wet grams	Check 1 grams	Check 2 grams	Dry grams	
1		Y / N					
2		Y / N					
3		Y / N					
4		Y / N					
Notes		Chamber Cleaned: Y / N	Oil Changed: Y / N	Maint. Needed: Y / N			

Batch #		Start Cooling	Trays In	Trays Out	Run Time	Extra Dry	Total
		am pm	am pm	am pm	hrs	hrs	hrs
Start Date:		Customize Temp	Time	Check Time:	am pm	am pm	am pm
End Date:		Freeze Dry		mTorr:			Subtract Dry from Wet for Water Loss
Tray Contents Description:	Examples: Raw, Cooked, Thickness, Liquid, Spread	Pre-Frozen	Wet grams	Check 1 grams	Check 2 grams	Dry grams	
1		Y / N					
2		Y / N					
3		Y / N					
4		Y / N					
Notes		Chamber Cleaned: Y / N	Oil Changed: Y / N	Maint. Needed: Y / N			

Batch #		Start Cooling	Trays In	Trays Out	Run Time	Extra Dry	Total
		am pm	am pm	am pm	hrs	hrs	hrs
Start Date:		Customize Temp	Time	Check Time:	am pm	am pm	am pm
End Date:		Freeze Dry		mTorr:			Subtract Dry from Wet for Water Loss
Tray Contents Description:	Examples: Raw, Cooked, Thickness, Liquid, Spread	Pre-Frozen	Wet grams	Check 1 grams	Check 2 grams	Dry grams	
1		Y / N					
2		Y / N					
3		Y / N					
4		Y / N					
Notes		Chamber Cleaned: Y / N	Oil Changed: Y / N	Maint. Needed: Y / N			

Keep track of how the foods process in your freeze-dryer.

Batch #		Start Cooling	Trays In	Trays Out	Run Time	Extra Dry	Total
		am pm	am pm	am pm	hrs	hrs	hrs
Start Date:		Customize	Temp	Time	Check Time:	am pm	am pm	am pm	Subtract Dry from Wet for Water Loss
End Date:		Freeze / Dry			mTorr:				
Tray Contents Description:	Examples: Raw, Cooked, Thickness, Liquid, Spread	Pre-Frozen	Wet grams	Check 1 grams	Check 2 grams	Dry grams	
1		Y / N					
2		Y / N					
3		Y / N					
4		Y / N					
Notes		Chamber Cleaned: Y / N	Oil Changed: Y / N	Maint. Needed: Y / N			

Batch #		Start Cooling	Trays In	Trays Out	Run Time	Extra Dry	Total
		am pm	am pm	am pm	hrs	hrs	hrs
Start Date:		Customize	Temp	Time	Check Time:	am pm	am pm	am pm	Subtract Dry from Wet for Water Loss
End Date:		Freeze / Dry			mTorr:				
Tray Contents Description:	Examples: Raw, Cooked, Thickness, Liquid, Spread	Pre-Frozen	Wet grams	Check 1 grams	Check 2 grams	Dry grams	
1		Y / N					
2		Y / N					
3		Y / N					
4		Y / N					
Notes		Chamber Cleaned: Y / N	Oil Changed: Y / N	Maint. Needed: Y / N			

Batch #		Start Cooling	Trays In	Trays Out	Run Time	Extra Dry	Total
		am pm	am pm	am pm	hrs	hrs	hrs
Start Date:		Customize	Temp	Time	Check Time:	am pm	am pm	am pm	Subtract Dry from Wet for Water Loss
End Date:		Freeze / Dry			mTorr:				
Tray Contents Description:	Examples: Raw, Cooked, Thickness, Liquid, Spread	Pre-Frozen	Wet grams	Check 1 grams	Check 2 grams	Dry grams	
1		Y / N					
2		Y / N					
3		Y / N					
4		Y / N					
Notes		Chamber Cleaned: Y / N	Oil Changed: Y / N	Maint. Needed: Y / N			

M   FREEZE-DRYER BATCH LOGS   PAGE#

Keep track of how the foods process in your freeze-dryer.

Batch #		Start Cooling	Trays In	Trays Out	Run Time	Extra Dry	Total
		am pm	am pm	am pm	hrs	hrs	hrs
Start Date:		Customize	Temp	Time	Check Time:	am pm	am pm	am pm	
End Date:		Freeze							Subtract Dry from Wet for Water Loss
		Dry			mTorr:				
Tray Contents Description:	Examples: Raw, Cooked, Thickness, Liquid, Spread		Pre-Frozen	Wet grams	Check 1 grams	Check 2 grams	Dry grams	
1			Y / N					
2			Y / N					
3			Y / N					
4			Y / N					
Notes			Chamber Cleaned: Y / N	Oil Changed: Y / N	Maint. Needed: Y / N		

Batch #		Start Cooling	Trays In	Trays Out	Run Time	Extra Dry	Total
		am pm	am pm	am pm	hrs	hrs	hrs
Start Date:		Customize	Temp	Time	Check Time:	am pm	am pm	am pm	
End Date:		Freeze							Subtract Dry from Wet for Water Loss
		Dry			mTorr:				
Tray Contents Description:	Examples: Raw, Cooked, Thickness, Liquid, Spread		Pre-Frozen	Wet grams	Check 1 grams	Check 2 grams	Dry grams	
1			Y / N					
2			Y / N					
3			Y / N					
4			Y / N					
Notes			Chamber Cleaned: Y / N	Oil Changed: Y / N	Maint. Needed: Y / N		

Batch #		Start Cooling	Trays In	Trays Out	Run Time	Extra Dry	Total
		am pm	am pm	am pm	hrs	hrs	hrs
Start Date:		Customize	Temp	Time	Check Time:	am pm	am pm	am pm	
End Date:		Freeze							Subtract Dry from Wet for Water Loss
		Dry			mTorr:				
Tray Contents Description:	Examples: Raw, Cooked, Thickness, Liquid, Spread		Pre-Frozen	Wet grams	Check 1 grams	Check 2 grams	Dry grams	
1			Y / N					
2			Y / N					
3			Y / N					
4			Y / N					
Notes			Chamber Cleaned: Y / N	Oil Changed: Y / N	Maint. Needed: Y / N		

M   FREEZE-DRYER BATCH LOGS

Keep track of how the foods process in your freeze-dryer.

Batch #		Start Cooling	Trays In	Trays Out	Run Time	Extra Dry	Total
		am pm	am pm	am pm	hrs	hrs	hrs
Start Date:		Customize Temp Time		Check Time:	am pm	am pm	am pm	
End Date:		Freeze						Subtract Dry from Wet for Water Loss
		Dry		mTorr:				
Tray Contents Description:	Examples: Raw, Cooked, Thickness, Liquid, Spread		Pre-Frozen	Wet grams	Check 1 grams	Check 2 grams	Dry grams	
1			Y / N					
2			Y / N					
3			Y / N					
4			Y / N					
Notes				Chamber Cleaned: Y / N	Oil Changed: Y / N	Maint. Needed: Y / N	

Batch #		Start Cooling	Trays In	Trays Out	Run Time	Extra Dry	Total
		am pm	am pm	am pm	hrs	hrs	hrs
Start Date:		Customize Temp Time		Check Time:	am pm	am pm	am pm	
End Date:		Freeze						Subtract Dry from Wet for Water Loss
		Dry		mTorr:				
Tray Contents Description:	Examples: Raw, Cooked, Thickness, Liquid, Spread		Pre-Frozen	Wet grams	Check 1 grams	Check 2 grams	Dry grams	
1			Y / N					
2			Y / N					
3			Y / N					
4			Y / N					
Notes				Chamber Cleaned: Y / N	Oil Changed: Y / N	Maint. Needed: Y / N	

Batch #		Start Cooling	Trays In	Trays Out	Run Time	Extra Dry	Total
		am pm	am pm	am pm	hrs	hrs	hrs
Start Date:		Customize Temp Time		Check Time:	am pm	am pm	am pm	
End Date:		Freeze						Subtract Dry from Wet for Water Loss
		Dry		mTorr:				
Tray Contents Description:	Examples: Raw, Cooked, Thickness, Liquid, Spread		Pre-Frozen	Wet grams	Check 1 grams	Check 2 grams	Dry grams	
1			Y / N					
2			Y / N					
3			Y / N					
4			Y / N					
Notes				Chamber Cleaned: Y / N	Oil Changed: Y / N	Maint. Needed: Y / N	

M   FREEZE-DRYER BATCH LOGS

Keep track of how the foods process in your freeze-dryer.

Batch #		Start Cooling	Trays In	Trays Out	Run Time	Extra Dry	Total
		am pm	am pm	am pm	hrs	hrs	hrs
Start Date:		Customize	Temp	Time	Check Time:	am pm	am pm	am pm	
End Date:		Freeze / Dry			mTorr:				Subtract Dry from Wet for Water Loss
Tray Contents Description:	Examples: Raw, Cooked, Thickness, Liquid, Spread	Pre-Frozen	Wet grams	Check 1 grams	Check 2 grams	Dry grams	
1		Y / N					
2		Y / N					
3		Y / N					
4		Y / N					
Notes		Chamber Cleaned: Y / N	Oil Changed: Y / N	Maint. Needed: Y / N			

Batch #		Start Cooling	Trays In	Trays Out	Run Time	Extra Dry	Total
		am pm	am pm	am pm	hrs	hrs	hrs
Start Date:		Customize	Temp	Time	Check Time:	am pm	am pm	am pm	
End Date:		Freeze / Dry			mTorr:				Subtract Dry from Wet for Water Loss
Tray Contents Description:	Examples: Raw, Cooked, Thickness, Liquid, Spread	Pre-Frozen	Wet grams	Check 1 grams	Check 2 grams	Dry grams	
1		Y / N					
2		Y / N					
3		Y / N					
4		Y / N					
Notes		Chamber Cleaned: Y / N	Oil Changed: Y / N	Maint. Needed: Y / N			

Batch #		Start Cooling	Trays In	Trays Out	Run Time	Extra Dry	Total
		am pm	am pm	am pm	hrs	hrs	hrs
Start Date:		Customize	Temp	Time	Check Time:	am pm	am pm	am pm	
End Date:		Freeze / Dry			mTorr:				Subtract Dry from Wet for Water Loss
Tray Contents Description:	Examples: Raw, Cooked, Thickness, Liquid, Spread	Pre-Frozen	Wet grams	Check 1 grams	Check 2 grams	Dry grams	
1		Y / N					
2		Y / N					
3		Y / N					
4		Y / N					
Notes		Chamber Cleaned: Y / N	Oil Changed: Y / N	Maint. Needed: Y / N			

Keep track of how the foods process in your freeze-dryer.

Batch #		Start Cooling	Trays In	Trays Out	Run Time	Extra Dry	Total
		am pm	am pm	am pm	hrs	hrs	hrs
Start Date:		Customize	Temp	Time	Check Time:	am pm	am pm	am pm	
End Date:		Freeze / Dry			mTorr:				Subtract Dry from Wet for Water Loss

Tray Contents Description:	Examples: Raw, Cooked, Thickness, Liquid, Spread	Pre-Frozen	Wet grams	Check 1 grams	Check 2 grams	Dry grams	
1		Y / N					
2		Y / N					
3		Y / N					
4		Y / N					
Notes		Chamber Cleaned: Y / N	Oil Changed: Y / N	Maint. Needed: Y / N			

Batch #		Start Cooling	Trays In	Trays Out	Run Time	Extra Dry	Total
		am pm	am pm	am pm	hrs	hrs	hrs
Start Date:		Customize	Temp	Time	Check Time:	am pm	am pm	am pm	
End Date:		Freeze / Dry			mTorr:				Subtract Dry from Wet for Water Loss

Tray Contents Description:	Examples: Raw, Cooked, Thickness, Liquid, Spread	Pre-Frozen	Wet grams	Check 1 grams	Check 2 grams	Dry grams	
1		Y / N					
2		Y / N					
3		Y / N					
4		Y / N					
Notes		Chamber Cleaned: Y / N	Oil Changed: Y / N	Maint. Needed: Y / N			

Batch #		Start Cooling	Trays In	Trays Out	Run Time	Extra Dry	Total
		am pm	am pm	am pm	hrs	hrs	hrs
Start Date:		Customize	Temp	Time	Check Time:	am pm	am pm	am pm	
End Date:		Freeze / Dry			mTorr:				Subtract Dry from Wet for Water Loss

Tray Contents Description:	Examples: Raw, Cooked, Thickness, Liquid, Spread	Pre-Frozen	Wet grams	Check 1 grams	Check 2 grams	Dry grams	
1		Y / N					
2		Y / N					
3		Y / N					
4		Y / N					
Notes		Chamber Cleaned: Y / N	Oil Changed: Y / N	Maint. Needed: Y / N			

Keep track of how the foods process in your freeze-dryer.

Batch #		Start Cooling	Trays In	Trays Out	Run Time	Extra Dry	Total
		am pm	am pm	am pm	hrs	hrs	hrs
Start Date:		Customize	Temp	Time	Check Time:	am pm	am pm	am pm	Subtract Dry from Wet for Water Loss
End Date:		Freeze Dry			mTorr:				
Tray Contents Description:	Examples: Raw, Cooked, Thickness, Liquid, Spread		Pre-Frozen	Wet grams	Check 1 grams	Check 2 grams	Dry grams	
1			Y / N					
2			Y / N					
3			Y / N					
4			Y / N					
Notes				Chamber Cleaned: Y / N	Oil Changed: Y / N	Maint. Needed: Y / N	

Batch #		Start Cooling	Trays In	Trays Out	Run Time	Extra Dry	Total
		am pm	am pm	am pm	hrs	hrs	hrs
Start Date:		Customize	Temp	Time	Check Time:	am pm	am pm	am pm	Subtract Dry from Wet for Water Loss
End Date:		Freeze Dry			mTorr:				
Tray Contents Description:	Examples: Raw, Cooked, Thickness, Liquid, Spread		Pre-Frozen	Wet grams	Check 1 grams	Check 2 grams	Dry grams	
1			Y / N					
2			Y / N					
3			Y / N					
4			Y / N					
Notes				Chamber Cleaned: Y / N	Oil Changed: Y / N	Maint. Needed: Y / N	

Batch #		Start Cooling	Trays In	Trays Out	Run Time	Extra Dry	Total
		am pm	am pm	am pm	hrs	hrs	hrs
Start Date:		Customize	Temp	Time	Check Time:	am pm	am pm	am pm	Subtract Dry from Wet for Water Loss
End Date:		Freeze Dry			mTorr:				
Tray Contents Description:	Examples: Raw, Cooked, Thickness, Liquid, Spread		Pre-Frozen	Wet grams	Check 1 grams	Check 2 grams	Dry grams	
1			Y / N					
2			Y / N					
3			Y / N					
4			Y / N					
Notes				Chamber Cleaned: Y / N	Oil Changed: Y / N	Maint. Needed: Y / N	

Keep track of how the foods process in your freeze-dryer.

Batch #		Start Cooling	Trays In	Trays Out	Run Time	Extra Dry	Total
		am pm	am pm	am pm	hrs	hrs	hrs
Start Date:		Customize Temp	Time	Check Time:	am pm	am pm	am pm
End Date:		Freeze Dry		mTorr:			Subtract Dry from Wet for Water Loss
Tray Contents Description:	Examples: Raw, Cooked, Thickness, Liquid, Spread	Pre-Frozen	Wet grams	Check 1 grams	Check 2 grams	Dry grams	
1		Y / N					
2		Y / N					
3		Y / N					
4		Y / N					
Notes			Chamber Cleaned: Y / N	Oil Changed: Y / N	Maint. Needed: Y / N		

Batch #		Start Cooling	Trays In	Trays Out	Run Time	Extra Dry	Total
		am pm	am pm	am pm	hrs	hrs	hrs
Start Date:		Customize Temp	Time	Check Time:	am pm	am pm	am pm
End Date:		Freeze Dry		mTorr:			Subtract Dry from Wet for Water Loss
Tray Contents Description:	Examples: Raw, Cooked, Thickness, Liquid, Spread	Pre-Frozen	Wet grams	Check 1 grams	Check 2 grams	Dry grams	
1		Y / N					
2		Y / N					
3		Y / N					
4		Y / N					
Notes			Chamber Cleaned: Y / N	Oil Changed: Y / N	Maint. Needed: Y / N		

Batch #		Start Cooling	Trays In	Trays Out	Run Time	Extra Dry	Total
		am pm	am pm	am pm	hrs	hrs	hrs
Start Date:		Customize Temp	Time	Check Time:	am pm	am pm	am pm
End Date:		Freeze Dry		mTorr:			Subtract Dry from Wet for Water Loss
Tray Contents Description:	Examples: Raw, Cooked, Thickness, Liquid, Spread	Pre-Frozen	Wet grams	Check 1 grams	Check 2 grams	Dry grams	
1		Y / N					
2		Y / N					
3		Y / N					
4		Y / N					
Notes			Chamber Cleaned: Y / N	Oil Changed: Y / N	Maint. Needed: Y / N		

Keep track of how the foods process in your freeze-dryer.

Batch #		Start Cooling	Trays In	Trays Out	Run Time	Extra Dry	Total
		am pm	am pm	am pm	hrs	hrs	hrs
Start Date:		Customize	Temp	Time	Check Time:	am pm	am pm	am pm	
End Date:		Freeze							Subtract Dry from Wet for Water Loss
		Dry			mTorr:				
Tray Contents Description:	Examples: Raw, Cooked, Thickness, Liquid, Spread	Pre-Frozen	Wet grams	Check 1 grams	Check 2 grams	Dry grams	
1		Y / N					
2		Y / N					
3		Y / N					
4		Y / N					
Notes		Chamber Cleaned: Y / N	Oil Changed: Y / N	Maint. Needed: Y / N			

Batch #		Start Cooling	Trays In	Trays Out	Run Time	Extra Dry	Total
		am pm	am pm	am pm	hrs	hrs	hrs
Start Date:		Customize	Temp	Time	Check Time:	am pm	am pm	am pm	
End Date:		Freeze							Subtract Dry from Wet for Water Loss
		Dry			mTorr:				
Tray Contents Description:	Examples: Raw, Cooked, Thickness, Liquid, Spread	Pre-Frozen	Wet grams	Check 1 grams	Check 2 grams	Dry grams	
1		Y / N					
2		Y / N					
3		Y / N					
4		Y / N					
Notes		Chamber Cleaned: Y / N	Oil Changed: Y / N	Maint. Needed: Y / N			

Batch #		Start Cooling	Trays In	Trays Out	Run Time	Extra Dry	Total
		am pm	am pm	am pm	hrs	hrs	hrs
Start Date:		Customize	Temp	Time	Check Time:	am pm	am pm	am pm	
End Date:		Freeze							Subtract Dry from Wet for Water Loss
		Dry			mTorr:				
Tray Contents Description:	Examples: Raw, Cooked, Thickness, Liquid, Spread	Pre-Frozen	Wet grams	Check 1 grams	Check 2 grams	Dry grams	
1		Y / N					
2		Y / N					
3		Y / N					
4		Y / N					
Notes		Chamber Cleaned: Y / N	Oil Changed: Y / N	Maint. Needed: Y / N			

M   FREEZE-DRYER BATCH LOGS

Keep track of how the foods process in your freeze-dryer.

Batch #		Start Cooling	Trays In	Trays Out	Run Time	Extra Dry	Total
		am / pm	am / pm	am / pm	hrs	hrs	hrs
Start Date:		Customize	Temp	Time	Check Time:	am / pm	am / pm	am / pm	
End Date:		Freeze							Subtract Dry from Wet for Water Loss
		Dry			mTorr:				
Tray Contents Description:	Examples: Raw, Cooked, Thickness, Liquid, Spread		Pre-Frozen	Wet grams	Check 1 grams	Check 2 grams	Dry grams	
1			Y / N					
2			Y / N					
3			Y / N					
4			Y / N					
Notes				Chamber Cleaned: Y / N	Oil Changed: Y / N	Maint. Needed: Y / N		

Batch #		Start Cooling	Trays In	Trays Out	Run Time	Extra Dry	Total
		am / pm	am / pm	am / pm	hrs	hrs	hrs
Start Date:		Customize	Temp	Time	Check Time:	am / pm	am / pm	am / pm	
End Date:		Freeze							Subtract Dry from Wet for Water Loss
		Dry			mTorr:				
Tray Contents Description:	Examples: Raw, Cooked, Thickness, Liquid, Spread		Pre-Frozen	Wet grams	Check 1 grams	Check 2 grams	Dry grams	
1			Y / N					
2			Y / N					
3			Y / N					
4			Y / N					
Notes				Chamber Cleaned: Y / N	Oil Changed: Y / N	Maint. Needed: Y / N		

Batch #		Start Cooling	Trays In	Trays Out	Run Time	Extra Dry	Total
		am / pm	am / pm	am / pm	hrs	hrs	hrs
Start Date:		Customize	Temp	Time	Check Time:	am / pm	am / pm	am / pm	
End Date:		Freeze							Subtract Dry from Wet for Water Loss
		Dry			mTorr:				
Tray Contents Description:	Examples: Raw, Cooked, Thickness, Liquid, Spread		Pre-Frozen	Wet grams	Check 1 grams	Check 2 grams	Dry grams	
1			Y / N					
2			Y / N					
3			Y / N					
4			Y / N					
Notes				Chamber Cleaned: Y / N	Oil Changed: Y / N	Maint. Needed: Y / N		

Keep track of how the foods process in your freeze-dryer.

Batch #		Start Cooling	Trays In	Trays Out	Run Time	Extra Dry	Total
		am pm	am pm	am pm	hrs	hrs	hrs
Start Date:		Customize Temp	Time	Check Time:	am pm	am pm	am pm
End Date:		Freeze					Subtract Dry from Wet for Water Loss
		Dry		mTorr:			
Tray Contents Description:	Examples: Raw, Cooked, Thickness, Liquid, Spread	Pre-Frozen	Wet grams	Check 1 grams	Check 2 grams	Dry grams	
1		Y / N					
2		Y / N					
3		Y / N					
4		Y / N					
Notes			Chamber Cleaned: Y / N	Oil Changed: Y / N	Maint. Needed: Y / N		

Batch #		Start Cooling	Trays In	Trays Out	Run Time	Extra Dry	Total
		am pm	am pm	am pm	hrs	hrs	hrs
Start Date:		Customize Temp	Time	Check Time:	am pm	am pm	am pm
End Date:		Freeze					Subtract Dry from Wet for Water Loss
		Dry		mTorr:			
Tray Contents Description:	Examples: Raw, Cooked, Thickness, Liquid, Spread	Pre-Frozen	Wet grams	Check 1 grams	Check 2 grams	Dry grams	
1		Y / N					
2		Y / N					
3		Y / N					
4		Y / N					
Notes			Chamber Cleaned: Y / N	Oil Changed: Y / N	Maint. Needed: Y / N		

Batch #		Start Cooling	Trays In	Trays Out	Run Time	Extra Dry	Total
		am pm	am pm	am pm	hrs	hrs	hrs
Start Date:		Customize Temp	Time	Check Time:	am pm	am pm	am pm
End Date:		Freeze					Subtract Dry from Wet for Water Loss
		Dry		mTorr:			
Tray Contents Description:	Examples: Raw, Cooked, Thickness, Liquid, Spread	Pre-Frozen	Wet grams	Check 1 grams	Check 2 grams	Dry grams	
1		Y / N					
2		Y / N					
3		Y / N					
4		Y / N					
Notes			Chamber Cleaned: Y / N	Oil Changed: Y / N	Maint. Needed: Y / N		

Keep track of how the foods process in your freeze-dryer.

Batch #		Start Cooling	Trays In	Trays Out	Run Time	Extra Dry	Total
		am pm	am pm	am pm	hrs	hrs	hrs
Start Date:		Customize	Temp	Time	Check Time:	am pm	am pm	am pm	
End Date:		Freeze Dry			mTorr:				Subtract Dry from Wet for Water Loss
Tray Contents Description:	Examples: Raw, Cooked, Thickness, Liquid, Spread		Pre-Frozen	Wet grams	Check 1 grams	Check 2 grams	Dry grams	
1			Y / N					
2			Y / N					
3			Y / N					
4			Y / N					
Notes				Chamber Cleaned: Y / N	Oil Changed: Y / N	Maint. Needed: Y / N	

Batch #		Start Cooling	Trays In	Trays Out	Run Time	Extra Dry	Total
		am pm	am pm	am pm	hrs	hrs	hrs
Start Date:		Customize	Temp	Time	Check Time:	am pm	am pm	am pm	
End Date:		Freeze Dry			mTorr:				Subtract Dry from Wet for Water Loss
Tray Contents Description:	Examples: Raw, Cooked, Thickness, Liquid, Spread		Pre-Frozen	Wet grams	Check 1 grams	Check 2 grams	Dry grams	
1			Y / N					
2			Y / N					
3			Y / N					
4			Y / N					
Notes				Chamber Cleaned: Y / N	Oil Changed: Y / N	Maint. Needed: Y / N	

Batch #		Start Cooling	Trays In	Trays Out	Run Time	Extra Dry	Total
		am pm	am pm	am pm	hrs	hrs	hrs
Start Date:		Customize	Temp	Time	Check Time:	am pm	am pm	am pm	
End Date:		Freeze Dry			mTorr:				Subtract Dry from Wet for Water Loss
Tray Contents Description:	Examples: Raw, Cooked, Thickness, Liquid, Spread		Pre-Frozen	Wet grams	Check 1 grams	Check 2 grams	Dry grams	
1			Y / N					
2			Y / N					
3			Y / N					
4			Y / N					
Notes				Chamber Cleaned: Y / N	Oil Changed: Y / N	Maint. Needed: Y / N	

Keep track of how the foods process in your freeze-dryer.

Batch #		Start Cooling	Trays In	Trays Out	Run Time	Extra Dry	Total
		am pm	am pm	am pm	hrs	hrs	hrs
Start Date:		Customize	Temp	Time	Check Time:	am pm	am pm	am pm	Subtract Dry from Wet for Water Loss
End Date:		Freeze Dry			mTorr:				
Tray Contents Description:	Examples: Raw, Cooked, Thickness, Liquid, Spread	Pre-Frozen	Wet grams	Check 1 grams	Check 2 grams	Dry grams	
1		Y / N					
2		Y / N					
3		Y / N					
4		Y / N					
Notes		Chamber Cleaned: Y / N	Oil Changed: Y / N	Maint. Needed: Y / N	

Batch #		Start Cooling	Trays In	Trays Out	Run Time	Extra Dry	Total
		am pm	am pm	am pm	hrs	hrs	hrs
Start Date:		Customize	Temp	Time	Check Time:	am pm	am pm	am pm	Subtract Dry from Wet for Water Loss
End Date:		Freeze Dry			mTorr:				
Tray Contents Description:	Examples: Raw, Cooked, Thickness, Liquid, Spread	Pre-Frozen	Wet grams	Check 1 grams	Check 2 grams	Dry grams	
1		Y / N					
2		Y / N					
3		Y / N					
4		Y / N					
Notes		Chamber Cleaned: Y / N	Oil Changed: Y / N	Maint. Needed: Y / N	

Batch #		Start Cooling	Trays In	Trays Out	Run Time	Extra Dry	Total
		am pm	am pm	am pm	hrs	hrs	hrs
Start Date:		Customize	Temp	Time	Check Time:	am pm	am pm	am pm	Subtract Dry from Wet for Water Loss
End Date:		Freeze Dry			mTorr:				
Tray Contents Description:	Examples: Raw, Cooked, Thickness, Liquid, Spread	Pre-Frozen	Wet grams	Check 1 grams	Check 2 grams	Dry grams	
1		Y / N					
2		Y / N					
3		Y / N					
4		Y / N					
Notes		Chamber Cleaned: Y / N	Oil Changed: Y / N	Maint. Needed: Y / N	

Keep track of how the foods process in your freeze-dryer.

Batch #		Start Cooling	Trays In	Trays Out	Run Time	Extra Dry	Total
		am pm	am pm	am pm	hrs	hrs	hrs
Start Date:		Customize Temp Time		Check Time:	am pm	am pm	am pm
End Date:		Freeze / Dry		mTorr:			Subtract Dry from Wet for Water Loss
Tray Contents Description:	Examples: Raw, Cooked, Thickness, Liquid, Spread	Pre-Frozen	Wet grams	Check 1 grams	Check 2 grams	Dry grams	
1		Y / N					
2		Y / N					
3		Y / N					
4		Y / N					
Notes		Chamber Cleaned: Y / N	Oil Changed: Y / N	Maint. Needed: Y / N			

Batch #		Start Cooling	Trays In	Trays Out	Run Time	Extra Dry	Total
		am pm	am pm	am pm	hrs	hrs	hrs
Start Date:		Customize Temp Time		Check Time:	am pm	am pm	am pm
End Date:		Freeze / Dry		mTorr:			Subtract Dry from Wet for Water Loss
Tray Contents Description:	Examples: Raw, Cooked, Thickness, Liquid, Spread	Pre-Frozen	Wet grams	Check 1 grams	Check 2 grams	Dry grams	
1		Y / N					
2		Y / N					
3		Y / N					
4		Y / N					
Notes		Chamber Cleaned: Y / N	Oil Changed: Y / N	Maint. Needed: Y / N			

Batch #		Start Cooling	Trays In	Trays Out	Run Time	Extra Dry	Total
		am pm	am pm	am pm	hrs	hrs	hrs
Start Date:		Customize Temp Time		Check Time:	am pm	am pm	am pm
End Date:		Freeze / Dry		mTorr:			Subtract Dry from Wet for Water Loss
Tray Contents Description:	Examples: Raw, Cooked, Thickness, Liquid, Spread	Pre-Frozen	Wet grams	Check 1 grams	Check 2 grams	Dry grams	
1		Y / N					
2		Y / N					
3		Y / N					
4		Y / N					
Notes		Chamber Cleaned: Y / N	Oil Changed: Y / N	Maint. Needed: Y / N			

M   FREEZE-DRYER BATCH LOGS

Keep track of how the foods process in your freeze-dryer.

Batch #		Start Cooling	Trays In	Trays Out	Run Time	Extra Dry	Total
		am pm	am pm	am pm	hrs	hrs	hrs
Start Date:		Customize Temp	Time	Check Time:	am pm	am pm	am pm
End Date:		Freeze					Subtract Dry from Wet for Water Loss
		Dry		mTorr:			
Tray Contents Description:	Examples: Raw, Cooked, Thickness, Liquid, Spread	Pre-Frozen	Wet grams	Check 1 grams	Check 2 grams	Dry grams	
1		Y / N					
2		Y / N					
3		Y / N					
4		Y / N					
Notes			Chamber Cleaned: Y / N	Oil Changed: Y / N	Maint. Needed: Y / N		

Batch #		Start Cooling	Trays In	Trays Out	Run Time	Extra Dry	Total
		am pm	am pm	am pm	hrs	hrs	hrs
Start Date:		Customize Temp	Time	Check Time:	am pm	am pm	am pm
End Date:		Freeze					Subtract Dry from Wet for Water Loss
		Dry		mTorr:			
Tray Contents Description:	Examples: Raw, Cooked, Thickness, Liquid, Spread	Pre-Frozen	Wet grams	Check 1 grams	Check 2 grams	Dry grams	
1		Y / N					
2		Y / N					
3		Y / N					
4		Y / N					
Notes			Chamber Cleaned: Y / N	Oil Changed: Y / N	Maint. Needed: Y / N		

Batch #		Start Cooling	Trays In	Trays Out	Run Time	Extra Dry	Total
		am pm	am pm	am pm	hrs	hrs	hrs
Start Date:		Customize Temp	Time	Check Time:	am pm	am pm	am pm
End Date:		Freeze					Subtract Dry from Wet for Water Loss
		Dry		mTorr:			
Tray Contents Description:	Examples: Raw, Cooked, Thickness, Liquid, Spread	Pre-Frozen	Wet grams	Check 1 grams	Check 2 grams	Dry grams	
1		Y / N					
2		Y / N					
3		Y / N					
4		Y / N					
Notes			Chamber Cleaned: Y / N	Oil Changed: Y / N	Maint. Needed: Y / N		

M   FREEZE-DRYER BATCH LOGS

Keep track of how the foods process in your freeze-dryer.

Batch #		Start Cooling	Trays In	Trays Out	Run Time	Extra Dry	Total
		am / pm	am / pm	am / pm	hrs	hrs	hrs
Start Date:		Customize	Temp	Time	Check Time:	am / pm	am / pm	am / pm	Subtract Dry from Wet for Water Loss
End Date:		Freeze / Dry			mTorr:				
Tray Contents Description:	Examples: Raw, Cooked, Thickness, Liquid, Spread	Pre-Frozen	Wet grams	Check 1 grams	Check 2 grams	Dry grams	
1		Y / N					
2		Y / N					
3		Y / N					
4		Y / N					
Notes		Chamber Cleaned: Y / N	Oil Changed: Y / N	Maint. Needed: Y / N			

Batch #		Start Cooling	Trays In	Trays Out	Run Time	Extra Dry	Total
		am / pm	am / pm	am / pm	hrs	hrs	hrs
Start Date:		Customize	Temp	Time	Check Time:	am / pm	am / pm	am / pm	Subtract Dry from Wet for Water Loss
End Date:		Freeze / Dry			mTorr:				
Tray Contents Description:	Examples: Raw, Cooked, Thickness, Liquid, Spread	Pre-Frozen	Wet grams	Check 1 grams	Check 2 grams	Dry grams	
1		Y / N					
2		Y / N					
3		Y / N					
4		Y / N					
Notes		Chamber Cleaned: Y / N	Oil Changed: Y / N	Maint. Needed: Y / N			

Batch #		Start Cooling	Trays In	Trays Out	Run Time	Extra Dry	Total
		am / pm	am / pm	am / pm	hrs	hrs	hrs
Start Date:		Customize	Temp	Time	Check Time:	am / pm	am / pm	am / pm	Subtract Dry from Wet for Water Loss
End Date:		Freeze / Dry			mTorr:				
Tray Contents Description:	Examples: Raw, Cooked, Thickness, Liquid, Spread	Pre-Frozen	Wet grams	Check 1 grams	Check 2 grams	Dry grams	
1		Y / N					
2		Y / N					
3		Y / N					
4		Y / N					
Notes		Chamber Cleaned: Y / N	Oil Changed: Y / N	Maint. Needed: Y / N			

M FREEZE-DRYER BATCH LOGS

Keep track of how the foods process in your freeze-dryer.

Batch 1

Batch #		Start Cooling	Trays In	Trays Out	Run Time	Extra Dry	Total
		am / pm	am / pm	am / pm	hrs	hrs	hrs
Start Date:		Customize	Temp	Time	Check Time:	am / pm	am / pm	am / pm	
End Date:		Freeze / Dry			mTorr:				Subtract Dry from Wet for Water Loss
Tray Contents Description:	Examples: Raw, Cooked, Thickness, Liquid, Spread		Pre-Frozen	Wet grams	Check 1 grams	Check 2 grams	Dry grams	
1			Y / N					
2			Y / N					
3			Y / N					
4			Y / N					
Notes				Chamber Cleaned: Y / N	Oil Changed: Y / N	Maint. Needed: Y / N	

Batch 2

Batch #		Start Cooling	Trays In	Trays Out	Run Time	Extra Dry	Total
		am / pm	am / pm	am / pm	hrs	hrs	hrs
Start Date:		Customize	Temp	Time	Check Time:	am / pm	am / pm	am / pm	
End Date:		Freeze / Dry			mTorr:				Subtract Dry from Wet for Water Loss
Tray Contents Description:	Examples: Raw, Cooked, Thickness, Liquid, Spread		Pre-Frozen	Wet grams	Check 1 grams	Check 2 grams	Dry grams	
1			Y / N					
2			Y / N					
3			Y / N					
4			Y / N					
Notes				Chamber Cleaned: Y / N	Oil Changed: Y / N	Maint. Needed: Y / N	

Batch 3

Batch #		Start Cooling	Trays In	Trays Out	Run Time	Extra Dry	Total
		am / pm	am / pm	am / pm	hrs	hrs	hrs
Start Date:		Customize	Temp	Time	Check Time:	am / pm	am / pm	am / pm	
End Date:		Freeze / Dry			mTorr:				Subtract Dry from Wet for Water Loss
Tray Contents Description:	Examples: Raw, Cooked, Thickness, Liquid, Spread		Pre-Frozen	Wet grams	Check 1 grams	Check 2 grams	Dry grams	
1			Y / N					
2			Y / N					
3			Y / N					
4			Y / N					
Notes				Chamber Cleaned: Y / N	Oil Changed: Y / N	Maint. Needed: Y / N	

Keep track of how the foods process in your freeze-dryer.

Batch #		Start Cooling	Trays In	Trays Out	Run Time	Extra Dry	Total
		am pm	am pm	am pm	hrs	hrs	hrs
Start Date:		Customize Temp	Time	Check Time:	am pm	am pm	am pm
End Date:		Freeze					Subtract Dry from Wet for Water Loss
		Dry		mTorr:			
Tray Contents Description:	Examples: Raw, Cooked, Thickness, Liquid, Spread		Pre-Frozen	Wet grams	Check 1 grams	Check 2 grams	Dry grams
1			Y / N				
2			Y / N				
3			Y / N				
4			Y / N				
Notes				Chamber Cleaned: Y / N	Oil Changed: Y / N	Maint. Needed: Y / N	

Batch #		Start Cooling	Trays In	Trays Out	Run Time	Extra Dry	Total
		am pm	am pm	am pm	hrs	hrs	hrs
Start Date:		Customize Temp	Time	Check Time:	am pm	am pm	am pm
End Date:		Freeze					Subtract Dry from Wet for Water Loss
		Dry		mTorr:			
Tray Contents Description:	Examples: Raw, Cooked, Thickness, Liquid, Spread		Pre-Frozen	Wet grams	Check 1 grams	Check 2 grams	Dry grams
1			Y / N				
2			Y / N				
3			Y / N				
4			Y / N				
Notes				Chamber Cleaned: Y / N	Oil Changed: Y / N	Maint. Needed: Y / N	

Batch #		Start Cooling	Trays In	Trays Out	Run Time	Extra Dry	Total
		am pm	am pm	am pm	hrs	hrs	hrs
Start Date:		Customize Temp	Time	Check Time:	am pm	am pm	am pm
End Date:		Freeze					Subtract Dry from Wet for Water Loss
		Dry		mTorr:			
Tray Contents Description:	Examples: Raw, Cooked, Thickness, Liquid, Spread		Pre-Frozen	Wet grams	Check 1 grams	Check 2 grams	Dry grams
1			Y / N				
2			Y / N				
3			Y / N				
4			Y / N				
Notes				Chamber Cleaned: Y / N	Oil Changed: Y / N	Maint. Needed: Y / N	

Keep track of how the foods process in your freeze-dryer.

Batch #		Start Cooling	Trays In	Trays Out	Run Time	Extra Dry	Total
		am pm	am pm	am pm	hrs	hrs	hrs
Start Date:		Customize	Temp	Time	Check Time:	am pm	am pm	am pm
End Date:		Freeze / Dry			mTorr:				Subtract Dry from Wet for Water Loss
Tray Contents Description:	Examples: Raw, Cooked, Thickness, Liquid, Spread	Pre-Frozen	Wet grams	Check 1 grams	Check 2 grams	Dry grams	
1		Y / N					
2		Y / N					
3		Y / N					
4		Y / N					
Notes			Chamber Cleaned: Y / N	Oil Changed: Y / N	Maint. Needed: Y / N		

Batch #		Start Cooling	Trays In	Trays Out	Run Time	Extra Dry	Total
		am pm	am pm	am pm	hrs	hrs	hrs
Start Date:		Customize	Temp	Time	Check Time:	am pm	am pm	am pm
End Date:		Freeze / Dry			mTorr:				Subtract Dry from Wet for Water Loss
Tray Contents Description:	Examples: Raw, Cooked, Thickness, Liquid, Spread	Pre-Frozen	Wet grams	Check 1 grams	Check 2 grams	Dry grams	
1		Y / N					
2		Y / N					
3		Y / N					
4		Y / N					
Notes			Chamber Cleaned: Y / N	Oil Changed: Y / N	Maint. Needed: Y / N		

Batch #		Start Cooling	Trays In	Trays Out	Run Time	Extra Dry	Total
		am pm	am pm	am pm	hrs	hrs	hrs
Start Date:		Customize	Temp	Time	Check Time:	am pm	am pm	am pm
End Date:		Freeze / Dry			mTorr:				Subtract Dry from Wet for Water Loss
Tray Contents Description:	Examples: Raw, Cooked, Thickness, Liquid, Spread	Pre-Frozen	Wet grams	Check 1 grams	Check 2 grams	Dry grams	
1		Y / N					
2		Y / N					
3		Y / N					
4		Y / N					
Notes			Chamber Cleaned: Y / N	Oil Changed: Y / N	Maint. Needed: Y / N		

Keep track of how the foods process in your freeze-dryer.

Batch #		Start Cooling	Trays In	Trays Out	Run Time	Extra Dry	Total
		am pm	am pm	am pm	hrs	hrs	hrs
Start Date:		Customize Temp	Time	Check Time:	am pm	am pm	am pm
End Date:		Freeze Dry		mTorr:			Subtract Dry from Wet for Water Loss
Tray Contents Description:	Examples: Raw, Cooked, Thickness, Liquid, Spread	Pre-Frozen	Wet grams	Check 1 grams	Check 2 grams	Dry grams	
1		Y / N					
2		Y / N					
3		Y / N					
4		Y / N					
Notes			Chamber Cleaned: Y / N	Oil Changed: Y / N	Maint. Needed: Y / N		

Batch #		Start Cooling	Trays In	Trays Out	Run Time	Extra Dry	Total
		am pm	am pm	am pm	hrs	hrs	hrs
Start Date:		Customize Temp	Time	Check Time:	am pm	am pm	am pm
End Date:		Freeze Dry		mTorr:			Subtract Dry from Wet for Water Loss
Tray Contents Description:	Examples: Raw, Cooked, Thickness, Liquid, Spread	Pre-Frozen	Wet grams	Check 1 grams	Check 2 grams	Dry grams	
1		Y / N					
2		Y / N					
3		Y / N					
4		Y / N					
Notes			Chamber Cleaned: Y / N	Oil Changed: Y / N	Maint. Needed: Y / N		

Batch #		Start Cooling	Trays In	Trays Out	Run Time	Extra Dry	Total
		am pm	am pm	am pm	hrs	hrs	hrs
Start Date:		Customize Temp	Time	Check Time:	am pm	am pm	am pm
End Date:		Freeze Dry		mTorr:			Subtract Dry from Wet for Water Loss
Tray Contents Description:	Examples: Raw, Cooked, Thickness, Liquid, Spread	Pre-Frozen	Wet grams	Check 1 grams	Check 2 grams	Dry grams	
1		Y / N					
2		Y / N					
3		Y / N					
4		Y / N					
Notes			Chamber Cleaned: Y / N	Oil Changed: Y / N	Maint. Needed: Y / N		

Keep track of how the foods process in your freeze-dryer.

Batch #		Start Cooling	Trays In	Trays Out	Run Time	Extra Dry	Total
		am pm	am pm	am pm	hrs	hrs	hrs
Start Date:		Customize	Temp	Time	Check Time:	am pm	am pm	am pm	
End Date:		Freeze Dry			mTorr:				Subtract Dry from Wet for Water Loss
Tray Contents Description:	Examples: Raw, Cooked, Thickness, Liquid, Spread		Pre-Frozen	Wet grams	Check 1 grams	Check 2 grams	Dry grams
1			Y / N				
2			Y / N				
3			Y / N				
4			Y / N				
Notes			Chamber Cleaned: Y / N	Oil Changed: Y / N	Maint. Needed: Y / N		

Batch #		Start Cooling	Trays In	Trays Out	Run Time	Extra Dry	Total
		am pm	am pm	am pm	hrs	hrs	hrs
Start Date:		Customize	Temp	Time	Check Time:	am pm	am pm	am pm	
End Date:		Freeze Dry			mTorr:				Subtract Dry from Wet for Water Loss
Tray Contents Description:	Examples: Raw, Cooked, Thickness, Liquid, Spread		Pre-Frozen	Wet grams	Check 1 grams	Check 2 grams	Dry grams
1			Y / N				
2			Y / N				
3			Y / N				
4			Y / N				
Notes			Chamber Cleaned: Y / N	Oil Changed: Y / N	Maint. Needed: Y / N		

Batch #		Start Cooling	Trays In	Trays Out	Run Time	Extra Dry	Total
		am pm	am pm	am pm	hrs	hrs	hrs
Start Date:		Customize	Temp	Time	Check Time:	am pm	am pm	am pm	
End Date:		Freeze Dry			mTorr:				Subtract Dry from Wet for Water Loss
Tray Contents Description:	Examples: Raw, Cooked, Thickness, Liquid, Spread		Pre-Frozen	Wet grams	Check 1 grams	Check 2 grams	Dry grams
1			Y / N				
2			Y / N				
3			Y / N				
4			Y / N				
Notes			Chamber Cleaned: Y / N	Oil Changed: Y / N	Maint. Needed: Y / N		

M   FREEZE-DRYER BATCH LOGS   PAGE#

Keep track of how the foods process in your freeze-dryer.

Batch 1

Batch #		Start Cooling	Trays In	Trays Out	Run Time	Extra Dry	Total
		am pm	am pm	am pm	hrs	hrs	hrs
Start Date:		Customize Temp	Time	Check Time:	am pm	am pm	am pm
End Date:		Freeze / Dry		mTorr:			Subtract Dry from Wet for Water Loss
Tray Contents Description:	Examples: Raw, Cooked, Thickness, Liquid, Spread		Pre-Frozen	Wet grams	Check 1 grams	Check 2 grams	Dry grams
1			Y / N				
2			Y / N				
3			Y / N				
4			Y / N				
Notes				Chamber Cleaned: Y / N	Oil Changed: Y / N	Maint. Needed: Y / N	

Batch 2

Batch #		Start Cooling	Trays In	Trays Out	Run Time	Extra Dry	Total
		am pm	am pm	am pm	hrs	hrs	hrs
Start Date:		Customize Temp	Time	Check Time:	am pm	am pm	am pm
End Date:		Freeze / Dry		mTorr:			Subtract Dry from Wet for Water Loss
Tray Contents Description:	Examples: Raw, Cooked, Thickness, Liquid, Spread		Pre-Frozen	Wet grams	Check 1 grams	Check 2 grams	Dry grams
1			Y / N				
2			Y / N				
3			Y / N				
4			Y / N				
Notes				Chamber Cleaned: Y / N	Oil Changed: Y / N	Maint. Needed: Y / N	

Batch 3

Batch #		Start Cooling	Trays In	Trays Out	Run Time	Extra Dry	Total
		am pm	am pm	am pm	hrs	hrs	hrs
Start Date:		Customize Temp	Time	Check Time:	am pm	am pm	am pm
End Date:		Freeze / Dry		mTorr:			Subtract Dry from Wet for Water Loss
Tray Contents Description:	Examples: Raw, Cooked, Thickness, Liquid, Spread		Pre-Frozen	Wet grams	Check 1 grams	Check 2 grams	Dry grams
1			Y / N				
2			Y / N				
3			Y / N				
4			Y / N				
Notes				Chamber Cleaned: Y / N	Oil Changed: Y / N	Maint. Needed: Y / N	

Keep track of how the foods process in your freeze-dryer.

Batch #		Start Cooling	Trays In	Trays Out	Run Time	Extra Dry	Total
		am pm	am pm	am pm	hrs	hrs	hrs
Start Date:		Customize Temp	Time	Check Time:	am pm	am pm	am pm
End Date:		Freeze / Dry		mTorr:			Subtract Dry from Wet for Water Loss
Tray Contents Description:	Examples: Raw, Cooked, Thickness, Liquid, Spread	Pre-Frozen	Wet grams	Check 1 grams	Check 2 grams	Dry grams	
1		Y / N					
2		Y / N					
3		Y / N					
4		Y / N					
Notes			Chamber Cleaned: Y / N	Oil Changed: Y / N	Maint. Needed: Y / N		

Batch #		Start Cooling	Trays In	Trays Out	Run Time	Extra Dry	Total
		am pm	am pm	am pm	hrs	hrs	hrs
Start Date:		Customize Temp	Time	Check Time:	am pm	am pm	am pm
End Date:		Freeze / Dry		mTorr:			Subtract Dry from Wet for Water Loss
Tray Contents Description:	Examples: Raw, Cooked, Thickness, Liquid, Spread	Pre-Frozen	Wet grams	Check 1 grams	Check 2 grams	Dry grams	
1		Y / N					
2		Y / N					
3		Y / N					
4		Y / N					
Notes			Chamber Cleaned: Y / N	Oil Changed: Y / N	Maint. Needed: Y / N		

Batch #		Start Cooling	Trays In	Trays Out	Run Time	Extra Dry	Total
		am pm	am pm	am pm	hrs	hrs	hrs
Start Date:		Customize Temp	Time	Check Time:	am pm	am pm	am pm
End Date:		Freeze / Dry		mTorr:			Subtract Dry from Wet for Water Loss
Tray Contents Description:	Examples: Raw, Cooked, Thickness, Liquid, Spread	Pre-Frozen	Wet grams	Check 1 grams	Check 2 grams	Dry grams	
1		Y / N					
2		Y / N					
3		Y / N					
4		Y / N					
Notes			Chamber Cleaned: Y / N	Oil Changed: Y / N	Maint. Needed: Y / N		

Keep track of how the foods process in your freeze-dryer.

Batch #		Start Cooling	Trays In	Trays Out	Run Time	Extra Dry	Total
		am pm	am pm	am pm	hrs	hrs	hrs
Start Date:		Customize Temp	Time	Check Time:	am pm	am pm	am pm
End Date:		Freeze Dry		mTorr:			Subtract Dry from Wet for Water Loss
Tray Contents Description:	Examples: Raw, Cooked, Thickness, Liquid, Spread	Pre-Frozen	Wet grams	Check 1 grams	Check 2 grams	Dry grams	
1		Y / N					
2		Y / N					
3		Y / N					
4		Y / N					
Notes			Chamber Cleaned: Y / N	Oil Changed: Y / N	Maint. Needed: Y / N		

Batch #		Start Cooling	Trays In	Trays Out	Run Time	Extra Dry	Total
		am pm	am pm	am pm	hrs	hrs	hrs
Start Date:		Customize Temp	Time	Check Time:	am pm	am pm	am pm
End Date:		Freeze Dry		mTorr:			Subtract Dry from Wet for Water Loss
Tray Contents Description:	Examples: Raw, Cooked, Thickness, Liquid, Spread	Pre-Frozen	Wet grams	Check 1 grams	Check 2 grams	Dry grams	
1		Y / N					
2		Y / N					
3		Y / N					
4		Y / N					
Notes			Chamber Cleaned: Y / N	Oil Changed: Y / N	Maint. Needed: Y / N		

Batch #		Start Cooling	Trays In	Trays Out	Run Time	Extra Dry	Total
		am pm	am pm	am pm	hrs	hrs	hrs
Start Date:		Customize Temp	Time	Check Time:	am pm	am pm	am pm
End Date:		Freeze Dry		mTorr:			Subtract Dry from Wet for Water Loss
Tray Contents Description:	Examples: Raw, Cooked, Thickness, Liquid, Spread	Pre-Frozen	Wet grams	Check 1 grams	Check 2 grams	Dry grams	
1		Y / N					
2		Y / N					
3		Y / N					
4		Y / N					
Notes			Chamber Cleaned: Y / N	Oil Changed: Y / N	Maint. Needed: Y / N		

Keep track of how the foods process in your freeze-dryer.

Batch #		Start Cooling	Trays In	Trays Out	Run Time	Extra Dry	Total
		am pm	am pm	am pm	hrs	hrs	hrs
Start Date:		Customize Temp	Time	Check Time:	am pm	am pm	am pm
End Date:		Freeze					
		Dry		mTorr:			Subtract Dry from Wet for Water Loss
Tray Contents Description:	Examples: Raw, Cooked, Thickness, Liquid, Spread	Pre-Frozen	Wet grams	Check 1 grams	Check 2 grams	Dry grams	
1		Y / N					
2		Y / N					
3		Y / N					
4		Y / N					
Notes			Chamber Cleaned: Y / N	Oil Changed: Y / N	Maint. Needed: Y / N		

Batch #		Start Cooling	Trays In	Trays Out	Run Time	Extra Dry	Total
		am pm	am pm	am pm	hrs	hrs	hrs
Start Date:		Customize Temp	Time	Check Time:	am pm	am pm	am pm
End Date:		Freeze					
		Dry		mTorr:			Subtract Dry from Wet for Water Loss
Tray Contents Description:	Examples: Raw, Cooked, Thickness, Liquid, Spread	Pre-Frozen	Wet grams	Check 1 grams	Check 2 grams	Dry grams	
1		Y / N					
2		Y / N					
3		Y / N					
4		Y / N					
Notes			Chamber Cleaned: Y / N	Oil Changed: Y / N	Maint. Needed: Y / N		

Batch #		Start Cooling	Trays In	Trays Out	Run Time	Extra Dry	Total
		am pm	am pm	am pm	hrs	hrs	hrs
Start Date:		Customize Temp	Time	Check Time:	am pm	am pm	am pm
End Date:		Freeze					
		Dry		mTorr:			Subtract Dry from Wet for Water Loss
Tray Contents Description:	Examples: Raw, Cooked, Thickness, Liquid, Spread	Pre-Frozen	Wet grams	Check 1 grams	Check 2 grams	Dry grams	
1		Y / N					
2		Y / N					
3		Y / N					
4		Y / N					
Notes			Chamber Cleaned: Y / N	Oil Changed: Y / N	Maint. Needed: Y / N		

Keep track of how the foods process in your freeze-dryer.

Batch #		Start Cooling	Trays In	Trays Out	Run Time	Extra Dry	Total
		am pm	am pm	am pm	hrs	hrs	hrs
Start Date:		Customize	Temp	Time	Check Time:	am pm	am pm	am pm	
End Date:		Freeze							Subtract Dry from Wet for Water Loss
		Dry			mTorr:				
Tray Contents Description:	Examples: Raw, Cooked, Thickness, Liquid, Spread		Pre-Frozen	Wet grams	Check 1 grams	Check 2 grams	Dry grams	
1			Y / N					
2			Y / N					
3			Y / N					
4			Y / N					
Notes				Chamber Cleaned: Y / N	Oil Changed: Y / N	Maint. Needed: Y / N		

Batch #		Start Cooling	Trays In	Trays Out	Run Time	Extra Dry	Total
		am pm	am pm	am pm	hrs	hrs	hrs
Start Date:		Customize	Temp	Time	Check Time:	am pm	am pm	am pm	
End Date:		Freeze							Subtract Dry from Wet for Water Loss
		Dry			mTorr:				
Tray Contents Description:	Examples: Raw, Cooked, Thickness, Liquid, Spread		Pre-Frozen	Wet grams	Check 1 grams	Check 2 grams	Dry grams	
1			Y / N					
2			Y / N					
3			Y / N					
4			Y / N					
Notes				Chamber Cleaned: Y / N	Oil Changed: Y / N	Maint. Needed: Y / N		

Batch #		Start Cooling	Trays In	Trays Out	Run Time	Extra Dry	Total
		am pm	am pm	am pm	hrs	hrs	hrs
Start Date:		Customize	Temp	Time	Check Time:	am pm	am pm	am pm	
End Date:		Freeze							Subtract Dry from Wet for Water Loss
		Dry			mTorr:				
Tray Contents Description:	Examples: Raw, Cooked, Thickness, Liquid, Spread		Pre-Frozen	Wet grams	Check 1 grams	Check 2 grams	Dry grams	
1			Y / N					
2			Y / N					
3			Y / N					
4			Y / N					
Notes				Chamber Cleaned: Y / N	Oil Changed: Y / N	Maint. Needed: Y / N		

Keep track of how the foods process in your freeze-dryer.

Batch 1

Batch #		Start Cooling	Trays In	Trays Out	Run Time	Extra Dry	Total
		am pm	am pm	am pm	hrs	hrs	hrs
Start Date:		Customize	Temp	Time	Check Time:	am pm	am pm	am pm	
End Date:		Freeze							Subtract Dry from Wet for Water Loss
		Dry			mTorr:				
Tray Contents Description:	Examples: Raw, Cooked, Thickness, Liquid, Spread		Pre-Frozen	Wet grams	Check 1 grams	Check 2 grams	Dry grams	
1			Y / N					
2			Y / N					
3			Y / N					
4			Y / N					
Notes			Chamber Cleaned: Y / N	Oil Changed: Y / N	Maint. Needed: Y / N		

Batch 2

Batch #		Start Cooling	Trays In	Trays Out	Run Time	Extra Dry	Total
		am pm	am pm	am pm	hrs	hrs	hrs
Start Date:		Customize	Temp	Time	Check Time:	am pm	am pm	am pm	
End Date:		Freeze							Subtract Dry from Wet for Water Loss
		Dry			mTorr:				
Tray Contents Description:	Examples: Raw, Cooked, Thickness, Liquid, Spread		Pre-Frozen	Wet grams	Check 1 grams	Check 2 grams	Dry grams	
1			Y / N					
2			Y / N					
3			Y / N					
4			Y / N					
Notes			Chamber Cleaned: Y / N	Oil Changed: Y / N	Maint. Needed: Y / N		

Batch 3

Batch #		Start Cooling	Trays In	Trays Out	Run Time	Extra Dry	Total
		am pm	am pm	am pm	hrs	hrs	hrs
Start Date:		Customize	Temp	Time	Check Time:	am pm	am pm	am pm	
End Date:		Freeze							Subtract Dry from Wet for Water Loss
		Dry			mTorr:				
Tray Contents Description:	Examples: Raw, Cooked, Thickness, Liquid, Spread		Pre-Frozen	Wet grams	Check 1 grams	Check 2 grams	Dry grams	
1			Y / N					
2			Y / N					
3			Y / N					
4			Y / N					
Notes			Chamber Cleaned: Y / N	Oil Changed: Y / N	Maint. Needed: Y / N		

Keep track of how the foods process in your freeze-dryer.

Batch #		Start Cooling	Trays In	Trays Out	Run Time	Extra Dry	Total
		am pm	am pm	am pm	hrs	hrs	hrs
Start Date:		Customize	Temp	Time	Check Time:	am pm	am pm	am pm	
End Date:		Freeze Dry			mTorr:				Subtract Dry from Wet for Water Loss
Tray Contents Description:	Examples: Raw, Cooked, Thickness, Liquid, Spread		Pre-Frozen	Wet grams	Check 1 grams	Check 2 grams	Dry grams	
1			Y / N					
2			Y / N					
3			Y / N					
4			Y / N					
Notes				Chamber Cleaned: Y / N	Oil Changed: Y / N	Maint. Needed: Y / N	

Batch #		Start Cooling	Trays In	Trays Out	Run Time	Extra Dry	Total
		am pm	am pm	am pm	hrs	hrs	hrs
Start Date:		Customize	Temp	Time	Check Time:	am pm	am pm	am pm	
End Date:		Freeze Dry			mTorr:				Subtract Dry from Wet for Water Loss
Tray Contents Description:	Examples: Raw, Cooked, Thickness, Liquid, Spread		Pre-Frozen	Wet grams	Check 1 grams	Check 2 grams	Dry grams	
1			Y / N					
2			Y / N					
3			Y / N					
4			Y / N					
Notes				Chamber Cleaned: Y / N	Oil Changed: Y / N	Maint. Needed: Y / N	

Batch #		Start Cooling	Trays In	Trays Out	Run Time	Extra Dry	Total
		am pm	am pm	am pm	hrs	hrs	hrs
Start Date:		Customize	Temp	Time	Check Time:	am pm	am pm	am pm	
End Date:		Freeze Dry			mTorr:				Subtract Dry from Wet for Water Loss
Tray Contents Description:	Examples: Raw, Cooked, Thickness, Liquid, Spread		Pre-Frozen	Wet grams	Check 1 grams	Check 2 grams	Dry grams	
1			Y / N					
2			Y / N					
3			Y / N					
4			Y / N					
Notes				Chamber Cleaned: Y / N	Oil Changed: Y / N	Maint. Needed: Y / N	

Keep track of how the foods process in your freeze-dryer.

Batch #		Start Cooling	Trays In	Trays Out	Run Time	Extra Dry	Total
		am pm	am pm	am pm	hrs	hrs	hrs
Start Date:		Customize	Temp	Time	Check Time:	am pm	am pm	am pm	
End Date:		Freeze							Subtract Dry from Wet for Water Loss
		Dry			mTorr:				
Tray Contents Description:	Examples: Raw, Cooked, Thickness, Liquid, Spread		Pre-Frozen	Wet grams	Check 1 grams	Check 2 grams	Dry grams	
1			Y / N					
2			Y / N					
3			Y / N					
4			Y / N					
Notes			Chamber Cleaned: Y / N	Oil Changed: Y / N	Maint. Needed: Y / N		

Batch #		Start Cooling	Trays In	Trays Out	Run Time	Extra Dry	Total
		am pm	am pm	am pm	hrs	hrs	hrs
Start Date:		Customize	Temp	Time	Check Time:	am pm	am pm	am pm	
End Date:		Freeze							Subtract Dry from Wet for Water Loss
		Dry			mTorr:				
Tray Contents Description:	Examples: Raw, Cooked, Thickness, Liquid, Spread		Pre-Frozen	Wet grams	Check 1 grams	Check 2 grams	Dry grams	
1			Y / N					
2			Y / N					
3			Y / N					
4			Y / N					
Notes			Chamber Cleaned: Y / N	Oil Changed: Y / N	Maint. Needed: Y / N		

Batch #		Start Cooling	Trays In	Trays Out	Run Time	Extra Dry	Total
		am pm	am pm	am pm	hrs	hrs	hrs
Start Date:		Customize	Temp	Time	Check Time:	am pm	am pm	am pm	
End Date:		Freeze							Subtract Dry from Wet for Water Loss
		Dry			mTorr:				
Tray Contents Description:	Examples: Raw, Cooked, Thickness, Liquid, Spread		Pre-Frozen	Wet grams	Check 1 grams	Check 2 grams	Dry grams	
1			Y / N					
2			Y / N					
3			Y / N					
4			Y / N					
Notes			Chamber Cleaned: Y / N	Oil Changed: Y / N	Maint. Needed: Y / N		

Keep track of how the foods process in your freeze-dryer.

Batch 1

Batch #		Start Cooling	Trays In	Trays Out	Run Time	Extra Dry	Total
		am / pm	am / pm	am / pm	hrs	hrs	hrs
Start Date:		Customize	Temp	Time	Check Time:	am / pm	am / pm	am / pm
End Date:		Freeze						Subtract Dry from Wet for Water Loss
		Dry			mTorr:			

Tray Contents Description:	Examples: Raw, Cooked, Thickness, Liquid, Spread	Pre-Frozen	Wet grams	Check 1 grams	Check 2 grams	Dry grams	
1		Y / N					
2		Y / N					
3		Y / N					
4		Y / N					

Notes	Chamber Cleaned: Y / N	Oil Changed: Y / N	Maint. Needed: Y / N

Batch 2

Batch #		Start Cooling	Trays In	Trays Out	Run Time	Extra Dry	Total
		am / pm	am / pm	am / pm	hrs	hrs	hrs
Start Date:		Customize	Temp	Time	Check Time:	am / pm	am / pm	am / pm
End Date:		Freeze						Subtract Dry from Wet for Water Loss
		Dry			mTorr:			

Tray Contents Description:	Examples: Raw, Cooked, Thickness, Liquid, Spread	Pre-Frozen	Wet grams	Check 1 grams	Check 2 grams	Dry grams	
1		Y / N					
2		Y / N					
3		Y / N					
4		Y / N					

Notes	Chamber Cleaned: Y / N	Oil Changed: Y / N	Maint. Needed: Y / N

Batch 3

Batch #		Start Cooling	Trays In	Trays Out	Run Time	Extra Dry	Total
		am / pm	am / pm	am / pm	hrs	hrs	hrs
Start Date:		Customize	Temp	Time	Check Time:	am / pm	am / pm	am / pm
End Date:		Freeze						Subtract Dry from Wet for Water Loss
		Dry			mTorr:			

Tray Contents Description:	Examples: Raw, Cooked, Thickness, Liquid, Spread	Pre-Frozen	Wet grams	Check 1 grams	Check 2 grams	Dry grams	
1		Y / N					
2		Y / N					
3		Y / N					
4		Y / N					

Notes	Chamber Cleaned: Y / N	Oil Changed: Y / N	Maint. Needed: Y / N

M   FREEZE-DRYER BATCH LOGS   PAGE#

Keep track of how the foods process in your freeze-dryer.

Batch 1

Batch #		Start Cooling	Trays In	Trays Out	Run Time	Extra Dry	Total
		am pm	am pm	am pm	hrs	hrs	hrs
Start Date:		Customize	Temp	Time	Check Time:	am pm	am pm	am pm	
End Date:		Freeze / Dry			mTorr:				Subtract Dry from Wet for Water Loss
Tray Contents Description:	Examples: Raw, Cooked, Thickness, Liquid, Spread		Pre-Frozen	Wet grams	Check 1 grams	Check 2 grams	Dry grams	
1			Y / N					
2			Y / N					
3			Y / N					
4			Y / N					
Notes			Chamber Cleaned: Y/N	Oil Changed: Y/N	Maint. Needed: Y/N		

Batch 2

Batch #		Start Cooling	Trays In	Trays Out	Run Time	Extra Dry	Total
		am pm	am pm	am pm	hrs	hrs	hrs
Start Date:		Customize	Temp	Time	Check Time:	am pm	am pm	am pm	
End Date:		Freeze / Dry			mTorr:				Subtract Dry from Wet for Water Loss
Tray Contents Description:	Examples: Raw, Cooked, Thickness, Liquid, Spread		Pre-Frozen	Wet grams	Check 1 grams	Check 2 grams	Dry grams	
1			Y / N					
2			Y / N					
3			Y / N					
4			Y / N					
Notes			Chamber Cleaned: Y/N	Oil Changed: Y/N	Maint. Needed: Y/N		

Batch 3

Batch #		Start Cooling	Trays In	Trays Out	Run Time	Extra Dry	Total
		am pm	am pm	am pm	hrs	hrs	hrs
Start Date:		Customize	Temp	Time	Check Time:	am pm	am pm	am pm	
End Date:		Freeze / Dry			mTorr:				Subtract Dry from Wet for Water Loss
Tray Contents Description:	Examples: Raw, Cooked, Thickness, Liquid, Spread		Pre-Frozen	Wet grams	Check 1 grams	Check 2 grams	Dry grams	
1			Y / N					
2			Y / N					
3			Y / N					
4			Y / N					
Notes			Chamber Cleaned: Y/N	Oil Changed: Y/N	Maint. Needed: Y/N		

M   FREEZE-DRYER BATCH LOGS

Keep track of how the foods process in your freeze-dryer.

Batch #		Start Cooling	Trays In	Trays Out	Run Time	Extra Dry	Total
		am pm	am pm	am pm	hrs	hrs	hrs
Start Date:		Customize Temp	Time	Check Time:	am pm	am pm	am pm
End Date:		Freeze					Subtract Dry from Wet for Water Loss
		Dry		mTorr:			
Tray Contents Description:	Examples: Raw, Cooked, Thickness, Liquid, Spread		Pre-Frozen	Wet grams	Check 1 grams	Check 2 grams	Dry grams
1			Y / N				
2			Y / N				
3			Y / N				
4			Y / N				
Notes			Chamber Cleaned: Y / N	Oil Changed: Y / N	Maint. Needed: Y / N		

Batch #		Start Cooling	Trays In	Trays Out	Run Time	Extra Dry	Total
		am pm	am pm	am pm	hrs	hrs	hrs
Start Date:		Customize Temp	Time	Check Time:	am pm	am pm	am pm
End Date:		Freeze					Subtract Dry from Wet for Water Loss
		Dry		mTorr:			
Tray Contents Description:	Examples: Raw, Cooked, Thickness, Liquid, Spread		Pre-Frozen	Wet grams	Check 1 grams	Check 2 grams	Dry grams
1			Y / N				
2			Y / N				
3			Y / N				
4			Y / N				
Notes			Chamber Cleaned: Y / N	Oil Changed: Y / N	Maint. Needed: Y / N		

Batch #		Start Cooling	Trays In	Trays Out	Run Time	Extra Dry	Total
		am pm	am pm	am pm	hrs	hrs	hrs
Start Date:		Customize Temp	Time	Check Time:	am pm	am pm	am pm
End Date:		Freeze					Subtract Dry from Wet for Water Loss
		Dry		mTorr:			
Tray Contents Description:	Examples: Raw, Cooked, Thickness, Liquid, Spread		Pre-Frozen	Wet grams	Check 1 grams	Check 2 grams	Dry grams
1			Y / N				
2			Y / N				
3			Y / N				
4			Y / N				
Notes			Chamber Cleaned: Y / N	Oil Changed: Y / N	Maint. Needed: Y / N		

Keep track of how the foods process in your freeze-dryer.

Batch #		Start Cooling	Trays In	Trays Out	Run Time	Extra Dry	Total
		am pm	am pm	am pm	hrs	hrs	hrs
Start Date:		Customize	Temp	Time	Check Time:	am pm	am pm	am pm	
End Date:		Freeze / Dry			mTorr:				Subtract Dry from Wet for Water Loss
Tray Contents Description:	Examples: Raw, Cooked, Thickness, Liquid, Spread		Pre-Frozen	Wet grams	Check 1 grams	Check 2 grams	Dry grams	
1			Y / N					
2			Y / N					
3			Y / N					
4			Y / N					
Notes			Chamber Cleaned: Y / N	Oil Changed: Y / N	Maint. Needed: Y / N		

Batch #		Start Cooling	Trays In	Trays Out	Run Time	Extra Dry	Total
		am pm	am pm	am pm	hrs	hrs	hrs
Start Date:		Customize	Temp	Time	Check Time:	am pm	am pm	am pm	
End Date:		Freeze / Dry			mTorr:				Subtract Dry from Wet for Water Loss
Tray Contents Description:	Examples: Raw, Cooked, Thickness, Liquid, Spread		Pre-Frozen	Wet grams	Check 1 grams	Check 2 grams	Dry grams	
1			Y / N					
2			Y / N					
3			Y / N					
4			Y / N					
Notes			Chamber Cleaned: Y / N	Oil Changed: Y / N	Maint. Needed: Y / N		

Batch #		Start Cooling	Trays In	Trays Out	Run Time	Extra Dry	Total
		am pm	am pm	am pm	hrs	hrs	hrs
Start Date:		Customize	Temp	Time	Check Time:	am pm	am pm	am pm	
End Date:		Freeze / Dry			mTorr:				Subtract Dry from Wet for Water Loss
Tray Contents Description:	Examples: Raw, Cooked, Thickness, Liquid, Spread		Pre-Frozen	Wet grams	Check 1 grams	Check 2 grams	Dry grams	
1			Y / N					
2			Y / N					
3			Y / N					
4			Y / N					
Notes			Chamber Cleaned: Y / N	Oil Changed: Y / N	Maint. Needed: Y / N		

M   FREEZE-DRYER BATCH LOGS   PAGE#

Keep track of how the foods process in your freeze-dryer.

Batch #		Start Cooling	Trays In	Trays Out	Run Time	Extra Dry	Total
		am pm	am pm	am pm	hrs	hrs	hrs
Start Date:		Customize	Temp	Time	Check Time:	am pm	am pm	am pm
End Date:		Freeze Dry			mTorr:				Subtract Dry from Wet for Water Loss
Tray Contents Description:	Examples: Raw, Cooked, Thickness, Liquid, Spread		Pre-Frozen	Wet grams	Check 1 grams	Check 2 grams	Dry grams	
1			Y / N					
2			Y / N					
3			Y / N					
4			Y / N					
Notes				Chamber Cleaned: Y / N	Oil Changed: Y / N	Maint. Needed: Y / N	

Batch #		Start Cooling	Trays In	Trays Out	Run Time	Extra Dry	Total
		am pm	am pm	am pm	hrs	hrs	hrs
Start Date:		Customize	Temp	Time	Check Time:	am pm	am pm	am pm
End Date:		Freeze Dry			mTorr:				Subtract Dry from Wet for Water Loss
Tray Contents Description:	Examples: Raw, Cooked, Thickness, Liquid, Spread		Pre-Frozen	Wet grams	Check 1 grams	Check 2 grams	Dry grams	
1			Y / N					
2			Y / N					
3			Y / N					
4			Y / N					
Notes				Chamber Cleaned: Y / N	Oil Changed: Y / N	Maint. Needed: Y / N	

Batch #		Start Cooling	Trays In	Trays Out	Run Time	Extra Dry	Total
		am pm	am pm	am pm	hrs	hrs	hrs
Start Date:		Customize	Temp	Time	Check Time:	am pm	am pm	am pm
End Date:		Freeze Dry			mTorr:				Subtract Dry from Wet for Water Loss
Tray Contents Description:	Examples: Raw, Cooked, Thickness, Liquid, Spread		Pre-Frozen	Wet grams	Check 1 grams	Check 2 grams	Dry grams	
1			Y / N					
2			Y / N					
3			Y / N					
4			Y / N					
Notes				Chamber Cleaned: Y / N	Oil Changed: Y / N	Maint. Needed: Y / N	

Keep track of how the foods process in your freeze-dryer.

Batch 1

Batch #		Start Cooling	Trays In	Trays Out	Run Time	Extra Dry	Total
		am pm	am pm	am pm	hrs	hrs	hrs
Start Date:		Customize	Temp	Time	Check Time:	am pm	am pm	am pm	
End Date:		Freeze							Subtract Dry from Wet for Water Loss
		Dry			mTorr:				
Tray Contents Description:	Examples: Raw, Cooked, Thickness, Liquid, Spread	Pre-Frozen	Wet grams	Check 1 grams	Check 2 grams	Dry grams	
1		Y / N					
2		Y / N					
3		Y / N					
4		Y / N					
Notes			Chamber Cleaned: Y / N	Oil Changed: Y / N	Maint. Needed: Y / N		

Batch 2

Batch #		Start Cooling	Trays In	Trays Out	Run Time	Extra Dry	Total
		am pm	am pm	am pm	hrs	hrs	hrs
Start Date:		Customize	Temp	Time	Check Time:	am pm	am pm	am pm	
End Date:		Freeze							Subtract Dry from Wet for Water Loss
		Dry			mTorr:				
Tray Contents Description:	Examples: Raw, Cooked, Thickness, Liquid, Spread	Pre-Frozen	Wet grams	Check 1 grams	Check 2 grams	Dry grams	
1		Y / N					
2		Y / N					
3		Y / N					
4		Y / N					
Notes			Chamber Cleaned: Y / N	Oil Changed: Y / N	Maint. Needed: Y / N		

Batch 3

Batch #		Start Cooling	Trays In	Trays Out	Run Time	Extra Dry	Total
		am pm	am pm	am pm	hrs	hrs	hrs
Start Date:		Customize	Temp	Time	Check Time:	am pm	am pm	am pm	
End Date:		Freeze							Subtract Dry from Wet for Water Loss
		Dry			mTorr:				
Tray Contents Description:	Examples: Raw, Cooked, Thickness, Liquid, Spread	Pre-Frozen	Wet grams	Check 1 grams	Check 2 grams	Dry grams	
1		Y / N					
2		Y / N					
3		Y / N					
4		Y / N					
Notes			Chamber Cleaned: Y / N	Oil Changed: Y / N	Maint. Needed: Y / N		

Keep track of how the foods process in your freeze-dryer.

Batch #		Start Cooling	Trays In	Trays Out	Run Time	Extra Dry	Total
		am pm	am pm	am pm	hrs	hrs	hrs
Start Date:		Customize	Temp	Time	Check Time:	am pm	am pm	am pm	
End Date:		Freeze Dry			mTorr:				Subtract Dry from Wet for Water Loss
Tray Contents Description:	Examples: Raw, Cooked, Thickness, Liquid, Spread		Pre-Frozen	Wet grams	Check 1 grams	Check 2 grams	Dry grams	
1			Y / N					
2			Y / N					
3			Y / N					
4			Y / N					
Notes			Chamber Cleaned: Y / N	Oil Changed: Y / N	Maint. Needed: Y / N		

Batch #		Start Cooling	Trays In	Trays Out	Run Time	Extra Dry	Total
		am pm	am pm	am pm	hrs	hrs	hrs
Start Date:		Customize	Temp	Time	Check Time:	am pm	am pm	am pm	
End Date:		Freeze Dry			mTorr:				Subtract Dry from Wet for Water Loss
Tray Contents Description:	Examples: Raw, Cooked, Thickness, Liquid, Spread		Pre-Frozen	Wet grams	Check 1 grams	Check 2 grams	Dry grams	
1			Y / N					
2			Y / N					
3			Y / N					
4			Y / N					
Notes			Chamber Cleaned: Y / N	Oil Changed: Y / N	Maint. Needed: Y / N		

Batch #		Start Cooling	Trays In	Trays Out	Run Time	Extra Dry	Total
		am pm	am pm	am pm	hrs	hrs	hrs
Start Date:		Customize	Temp	Time	Check Time:	am pm	am pm	am pm	
End Date:		Freeze Dry			mTorr:				Subtract Dry from Wet for Water Loss
Tray Contents Description:	Examples: Raw, Cooked, Thickness, Liquid, Spread		Pre-Frozen	Wet grams	Check 1 grams	Check 2 grams	Dry grams	
1			Y / N					
2			Y / N					
3			Y / N					
4			Y / N					
Notes			Chamber Cleaned: Y / N	Oil Changed: Y / N	Maint. Needed: Y / N		

M FREEZE-DRYER BATCH LOGS PAGE#

Keep track of how the foods process in your freeze-dryer.

Batch #		Start Cooling	Trays In	Trays Out	Run Time	Extra Dry	Total
		am pm	am pm	am pm	hrs	hrs	hrs
Start Date:		Customize Temp Time		Check Time:	am pm	am pm	am pm	
End Date:		Freeze						Subtract Dry from Wet for Water Loss
		Dry		mTorr:				
Tray Contents Description:	Examples: Raw, Cooked, Thickness, Liquid, Spread	Pre-Frozen	Wet grams	Check 1 grams	Check 2 grams	Dry grams	
1		Y / N					
2		Y / N					
3		Y / N					
4		Y / N					
Notes		Chamber Cleaned: Y / N	Oil Changed: Y / N	Maint. Needed: Y / N			

Batch #		Start Cooling	Trays In	Trays Out	Run Time	Extra Dry	Total
		am pm	am pm	am pm	hrs	hrs	hrs
Start Date:		Customize Temp Time		Check Time:	am pm	am pm	am pm	
End Date:		Freeze						Subtract Dry from Wet for Water Loss
		Dry		mTorr:				
Tray Contents Description:	Examples: Raw, Cooked, Thickness, Liquid, Spread	Pre-Frozen	Wet grams	Check 1 grams	Check 2 grams	Dry grams	
1		Y / N					
2		Y / N					
3		Y / N					
4		Y / N					
Notes		Chamber Cleaned: Y / N	Oil Changed: Y / N	Maint. Needed: Y / N			

Batch #		Start Cooling	Trays In	Trays Out	Run Time	Extra Dry	Total
		am pm	am pm	am pm	hrs	hrs	hrs
Start Date:		Customize Temp Time		Check Time:	am pm	am pm	am pm	
End Date:		Freeze						Subtract Dry from Wet for Water Loss
		Dry		mTorr:				
Tray Contents Description:	Examples: Raw, Cooked, Thickness, Liquid, Spread	Pre-Frozen	Wet grams	Check 1 grams	Check 2 grams	Dry grams	
1		Y / N					
2		Y / N					
3		Y / N					
4		Y / N					
Notes		Chamber Cleaned: Y / N	Oil Changed: Y / N	Maint. Needed: Y / N			

M   FREEZE-DRYER BATCH LOGS   PAGE#

Keep track of how the foods process in your freeze-dryer.

Batch #		Start Cooling	Trays In	Trays Out	Run Time	Extra Dry	Total
		am pm	am pm	am pm	hrs	hrs	hrs
Start Date:		Customize	Temp	Time	Check Time:	am pm	am pm	am pm
End Date:		Freeze							Subtract Dry from Wet for Water Loss
		Dry			mTorr:			
Tray Contents Description:	Examples: Raw, Cooked, Thickness, Liquid, Spread	Pre-Frozen	Wet grams	Check 1 grams	Check 2 grams	Dry grams	
1		Y / N					
2		Y / N					
3		Y / N					
4		Y / N					
Notes		Chamber Cleaned: Y / N	Oil Changed: Y / N	Maint. Needed: Y / N			

Batch #		Start Cooling	Trays In	Trays Out	Run Time	Extra Dry	Total
		am pm	am pm	am pm	hrs	hrs	hrs
Start Date:		Customize	Temp	Time	Check Time:	am pm	am pm	am pm
End Date:		Freeze							Subtract Dry from Wet for Water Loss
		Dry			mTorr:			
Tray Contents Description:	Examples: Raw, Cooked, Thickness, Liquid, Spread	Pre-Frozen	Wet grams	Check 1 grams	Check 2 grams	Dry grams	
1		Y / N					
2		Y / N					
3		Y / N					
4		Y / N					
Notes		Chamber Cleaned: Y / N	Oil Changed: Y / N	Maint. Needed: Y / N			

Batch #		Start Cooling	Trays In	Trays Out	Run Time	Extra Dry	Total
		am pm	am pm	am pm	hrs	hrs	hrs
Start Date:		Customize	Temp	Time	Check Time:	am pm	am pm	am pm
End Date:		Freeze							Subtract Dry from Wet for Water Loss
		Dry			mTorr:			
Tray Contents Description:	Examples: Raw, Cooked, Thickness, Liquid, Spread	Pre-Frozen	Wet grams	Check 1 grams	Check 2 grams	Dry grams	
1		Y / N					
2		Y / N					
3		Y / N					
4		Y / N					
Notes		Chamber Cleaned: Y / N	Oil Changed: Y / N	Maint. Needed: Y / N			

Keep track of how the foods process in your freeze-dryer.

Batch #		Start Cooling	Trays In	Trays Out	Run Time	Extra Dry	Total
		am pm	am pm	am pm	hrs	hrs	hrs
Start Date:		Customize	Temp	Time	Check Time:	am pm	am pm	am pm	
End Date:		Freeze							Subtract Dry from Wet for Water Loss
		Dry			mTorr:				
Tray Contents Description:	Examples: Raw, Cooked, Thickness, Liquid, Spread	Pre-Frozen	Wet grams	Check 1 grams	Check 2 grams	Dry grams	
1		Y / N					
2		Y / N					
3		Y / N					
4		Y / N					
Notes		Chamber Cleaned: Y / N	Oil Changed: Y / N	Maint. Needed: Y / N			

Batch #		Start Cooling	Trays In	Trays Out	Run Time	Extra Dry	Total
		am pm	am pm	am pm	hrs	hrs	hrs
Start Date:		Customize	Temp	Time	Check Time:	am pm	am pm	am pm	
End Date:		Freeze							Subtract Dry from Wet for Water Loss
		Dry			mTorr:				
Tray Contents Description:	Examples: Raw, Cooked, Thickness, Liquid, Spread	Pre-Frozen	Wet grams	Check 1 grams	Check 2 grams	Dry grams	
1		Y / N					
2		Y / N					
3		Y / N					
4		Y / N					
Notes		Chamber Cleaned: Y / N	Oil Changed: Y / N	Maint. Needed: Y / N			

Batch #		Start Cooling	Trays In	Trays Out	Run Time	Extra Dry	Total
		am pm	am pm	am pm	hrs	hrs	hrs
Start Date:		Customize	Temp	Time	Check Time:	am pm	am pm	am pm	
End Date:		Freeze							Subtract Dry from Wet for Water Loss
		Dry			mTorr:				
Tray Contents Description:	Examples: Raw, Cooked, Thickness, Liquid, Spread	Pre-Frozen	Wet grams	Check 1 grams	Check 2 grams	Dry grams	
1		Y / N					
2		Y / N					
3		Y / N					
4		Y / N					
Notes		Chamber Cleaned: Y / N	Oil Changed: Y / N	Maint. Needed: Y / N			

M FREEZE-DRYER BATCH LOGS

Keep track of how the foods process in your freeze-dryer.

Batch #		Start Cooling	Trays In	Trays Out	Run Time	Extra Dry	Total
		am / pm	am / pm	am / pm	hrs	hrs	hrs
Start Date:		Customize	Temp	Time	Check Time:	am / pm	am / pm	am / pm	
End Date:		Freeze							Subtract Dry from Wet for Water Loss
		Dry			mTorr:				
Tray Contents Description:	Examples: Raw, Cooked, Thickness, Liquid, Spread	Pre-Frozen	Wet grams	Check 1 grams	Check 2 grams	Dry grams	
1		Y / N					
2		Y / N					
3		Y / N					
4		Y / N					
Notes		Chamber Cleaned: Y / N	Oil Changed: Y / N	Maint. Needed: Y / N	

Batch #		Start Cooling	Trays In	Trays Out	Run Time	Extra Dry	Total
		am / pm	am / pm	am / pm	hrs	hrs	hrs
Start Date:		Customize	Temp	Time	Check Time:	am / pm	am / pm	am / pm	
End Date:		Freeze							Subtract Dry from Wet for Water Loss
		Dry			mTorr:				
Tray Contents Description:	Examples: Raw, Cooked, Thickness, Liquid, Spread	Pre-Frozen	Wet grams	Check 1 grams	Check 2 grams	Dry grams	
1		Y / N					
2		Y / N					
3		Y / N					
4		Y / N					
Notes		Chamber Cleaned: Y / N	Oil Changed: Y / N	Maint. Needed: Y / N	

Batch #		Start Cooling	Trays In	Trays Out	Run Time	Extra Dry	Total
		am / pm	am / pm	am / pm	hrs	hrs	hrs
Start Date:		Customize	Temp	Time	Check Time:	am / pm	am / pm	am / pm	
End Date:		Freeze							Subtract Dry from Wet for Water Loss
		Dry			mTorr:				
Tray Contents Description:	Examples: Raw, Cooked, Thickness, Liquid, Spread	Pre-Frozen	Wet grams	Check 1 grams	Check 2 grams	Dry grams	
1		Y / N					
2		Y / N					
3		Y / N					
4		Y / N					
Notes		Chamber Cleaned: Y / N	Oil Changed: Y / N	Maint. Needed: Y / N	

M FREEZE-DRYER BATCH LOGS PAGE#

Keep track of how the foods process in your freeze-dryer.

Batch #		Start Cooling	Trays In	Trays Out	Run Time	Extra Dry	Total
		am pm	am pm	am pm	hrs	hrs	hrs
Start Date:		Customize Temp	Time	Check Time:	am pm	am pm	am pm
End Date:		Freeze Dry		mTorr:			Subtract Dry from Wet for Water Loss
Tray Contents Description:	Examples: Raw, Cooked, Thickness, Liquid, Spread	Pre-Frozen	Wet grams	Check 1 grams	Check 2 grams	Dry grams	
1		Y / N					
2		Y / N					
3		Y / N					
4		Y / N					
Notes			Chamber Cleaned: Y / N	Oil Changed: Y / N	Maint. Needed: Y / N		

Batch #		Start Cooling	Trays In	Trays Out	Run Time	Extra Dry	Total
		am pm	am pm	am pm	hrs	hrs	hrs
Start Date:		Customize Temp	Time	Check Time:	am pm	am pm	am pm
End Date:		Freeze Dry		mTorr:			Subtract Dry from Wet for Water Loss
Tray Contents Description:	Examples: Raw, Cooked, Thickness, Liquid, Spread	Pre-Frozen	Wet grams	Check 1 grams	Check 2 grams	Dry grams	
1		Y / N					
2		Y / N					
3		Y / N					
4		Y / N					
Notes			Chamber Cleaned: Y / N	Oil Changed: Y / N	Maint. Needed: Y / N		

Batch #		Start Cooling	Trays In	Trays Out	Run Time	Extra Dry	Total
		am pm	am pm	am pm	hrs	hrs	hrs
Start Date:		Customize Temp	Time	Check Time:	am pm	am pm	am pm
End Date:		Freeze Dry		mTorr:			Subtract Dry from Wet for Water Loss
Tray Contents Description:	Examples: Raw, Cooked, Thickness, Liquid, Spread	Pre-Frozen	Wet grams	Check 1 grams	Check 2 grams	Dry grams	
1		Y / N					
2		Y / N					
3		Y / N					
4		Y / N					
Notes			Chamber Cleaned: Y / N	Oil Changed: Y / N	Maint. Needed: Y / N		

M FREEZE-DRYER BATCH LOGS

Keep track of how the foods process in your freeze-dryer.

Batch #		Start Cooling	Trays In	Trays Out	Run Time	Extra Dry	Total
		am pm	am pm	am pm	hrs	hrs	hrs
Start Date:		Customize	Temp	Time	Check Time:	am pm	am pm	am pm	
End Date:		Freeze							Subtract Dry from Wet for Water Loss
		Dry			mTorr:				
Tray Contents Description:	Examples: Raw, Cooked, Thickness, Liquid, Spread		Pre-Frozen	Wet grams	Check 1 grams	Check 2 grams	Dry grams	
1			Y / N					
2			Y / N					
3			Y / N					
4			Y / N					
Notes				Chamber Cleaned: Y / N	Oil Changed: Y / N	Maint. Needed: Y / N	

Batch #		Start Cooling	Trays In	Trays Out	Run Time	Extra Dry	Total
		am pm	am pm	am pm	hrs	hrs	hrs
Start Date:		Customize	Temp	Time	Check Time:	am pm	am pm	am pm	
End Date:		Freeze							Subtract Dry from Wet for Water Loss
		Dry			mTorr:				
Tray Contents Description:	Examples: Raw, Cooked, Thickness, Liquid, Spread		Pre-Frozen	Wet grams	Check 1 grams	Check 2 grams	Dry grams	
1			Y / N					
2			Y / N					
3			Y / N					
4			Y / N					
Notes				Chamber Cleaned: Y / N	Oil Changed: Y / N	Maint. Needed: Y / N	

Batch #		Start Cooling	Trays In	Trays Out	Run Time	Extra Dry	Total
		am pm	am pm	am pm	hrs	hrs	hrs
Start Date:		Customize	Temp	Time	Check Time:	am pm	am pm	am pm	
End Date:		Freeze							Subtract Dry from Wet for Water Loss
		Dry			mTorr:				
Tray Contents Description:	Examples: Raw, Cooked, Thickness, Liquid, Spread		Pre-Frozen	Wet grams	Check 1 grams	Check 2 grams	Dry grams	
1			Y / N					
2			Y / N					
3			Y / N					
4			Y / N					
Notes				Chamber Cleaned: Y / N	Oil Changed: Y / N	Maint. Needed: Y / N	

M FREEZE-DRYER BATCH LOGS

Keep track of how the foods process in your freeze-dryer.

Batch #		Start Cooling	Trays In	Trays Out	Run Time	Extra Dry	Total
		am pm	am pm	am pm	hrs	hrs	hrs
Start Date:		Customize	Temp	Time	Check Time:	am pm	am pm	am pm	
End Date:		Freeze							Subtract Dry from Wet for Water Loss
		Dry			mTorr:				
Tray Contents Description:	Examples: Raw, Cooked, Thickness, Liquid, Spread		Pre-Frozen	Wet grams	Check 1 grams	Check 2 grams	Dry grams	
1			Y / N					
2			Y / N					
3			Y / N					
4			Y / N					
Notes			Chamber Cleaned: Y / N	Oil Changed: Y / N	Maint. Needed: Y / N		

Batch #		Start Cooling	Trays In	Trays Out	Run Time	Extra Dry	Total
		am pm	am pm	am pm	hrs	hrs	hrs
Start Date:		Customize	Temp	Time	Check Time:	am pm	am pm	am pm	
End Date:		Freeze							Subtract Dry from Wet for Water Loss
		Dry			mTorr:				
Tray Contents Description:	Examples: Raw, Cooked, Thickness, Liquid, Spread		Pre-Frozen	Wet grams	Check 1 grams	Check 2 grams	Dry grams	
1			Y / N					
2			Y / N					
3			Y / N					
4			Y / N					
Notes			Chamber Cleaned: Y / N	Oil Changed: Y / N	Maint. Needed: Y / N		

Batch #		Start Cooling	Trays In	Trays Out	Run Time	Extra Dry	Total
		am pm	am pm	am pm	hrs	hrs	hrs
Start Date:		Customize	Temp	Time	Check Time:	am pm	am pm	am pm	
End Date:		Freeze							Subtract Dry from Wet for Water Loss
		Dry			mTorr:				
Tray Contents Description:	Examples: Raw, Cooked, Thickness, Liquid, Spread		Pre-Frozen	Wet grams	Check 1 grams	Check 2 grams	Dry grams	
1			Y / N					
2			Y / N					
3			Y / N					
4			Y / N					
Notes			Chamber Cleaned: Y / N	Oil Changed: Y / N	Maint. Needed: Y / N		

M FREEZE-DRYER BATCH LOGS

Keep track of how the foods process in your freeze-dryer.

Batch #		Start Cooling	Trays In	Trays Out	Run Time	Extra Dry	Total
		am / pm	am / pm	am / pm	hrs	hrs	hrs
Start Date:		Customize	Temp	Time	Check Time:	am / pm	am / pm	am / pm	Subtract Dry from Wet for Water Loss
End Date:		Freeze / Dry			mTorr:				
Tray Contents Description:	Examples: Raw, Cooked, Thickness, Liquid, Spread	Pre-Frozen	Wet grams	Check 1 grams	Check 2 grams	Dry grams	
1		Y / N					
2		Y / N					
3		Y / N					
4		Y / N					
Notes			Chamber Cleaned: Y / N	Oil Changed: Y / N	Maint. Needed: Y / N	

Batch #		Start Cooling	Trays In	Trays Out	Run Time	Extra Dry	Total
		am / pm	am / pm	am / pm	hrs	hrs	hrs
Start Date:		Customize	Temp	Time	Check Time:	am / pm	am / pm	am / pm	Subtract Dry from Wet for Water Loss
End Date:		Freeze / Dry			mTorr:				
Tray Contents Description:	Examples: Raw, Cooked, Thickness, Liquid, Spread	Pre-Frozen	Wet grams	Check 1 grams	Check 2 grams	Dry grams	
1		Y / N					
2		Y / N					
3		Y / N					
4		Y / N					
Notes			Chamber Cleaned: Y / N	Oil Changed: Y / N	Maint. Needed: Y / N	

Batch #		Start Cooling	Trays In	Trays Out	Run Time	Extra Dry	Total
		am / pm	am / pm	am / pm	hrs	hrs	hrs
Start Date:		Customize	Temp	Time	Check Time:	am / pm	am / pm	am / pm	Subtract Dry from Wet for Water Loss
End Date:		Freeze / Dry			mTorr:				
Tray Contents Description:	Examples: Raw, Cooked, Thickness, Liquid, Spread	Pre-Frozen	Wet grams	Check 1 grams	Check 2 grams	Dry grams	
1		Y / N					
2		Y / N					
3		Y / N					
4		Y / N					
Notes			Chamber Cleaned: Y / N	Oil Changed: Y / N	Maint. Needed: Y / N	

M FREEZE-DRYER BATCH LOGS

Keep track of how the foods process in your freeze-dryer.

Batch #		Start Cooling	Trays In	Trays Out	Run Time	Extra Dry	Total
		am pm	am pm	am pm	hrs	hrs	hrs
Start Date:		Customize Temp Time			Check Time:	am pm	am pm	am pm	Subtract Dry from Wet for Water Loss
End Date:		Freeze							
		Dry			mTorr:				
Tray Contents Description:	Examples: Raw, Cooked, Thickness, Liquid, Spread		Pre-Frozen	Wet grams	Check 1 grams	Check 2 grams	Dry grams	
1			Y / N					
2			Y / N					
3			Y / N					
4			Y / N					
Notes				Chamber Cleaned: Y / N	Oil Changed: Y / N	Maint. Needed: Y / N	

Batch #		Start Cooling	Trays In	Trays Out	Run Time	Extra Dry	Total
		am pm	am pm	am pm	hrs	hrs	hrs
Start Date:		Customize Temp Time			Check Time:	am pm	am pm	am pm	Subtract Dry from Wet for Water Loss
End Date:		Freeze							
		Dry			mTorr:				
Tray Contents Description:	Examples: Raw, Cooked, Thickness, Liquid, Spread		Pre-Frozen	Wet grams	Check 1 grams	Check 2 grams	Dry grams	
1			Y / N					
2			Y / N					
3			Y / N					
4			Y / N					
Notes				Chamber Cleaned: Y / N	Oil Changed: Y / N	Maint. Needed: Y / N	

Batch #		Start Cooling	Trays In	Trays Out	Run Time	Extra Dry	Total
		am pm	am pm	am pm	hrs	hrs	hrs
Start Date:		Customize Temp Time			Check Time:	am pm	am pm	am pm	Subtract Dry from Wet for Water Loss
End Date:		Freeze							
		Dry			mTorr:				
Tray Contents Description:	Examples: Raw, Cooked, Thickness, Liquid, Spread		Pre-Frozen	Wet grams	Check 1 grams	Check 2 grams	Dry grams	
1			Y / N					
2			Y / N					
3			Y / N					
4			Y / N					
Notes				Chamber Cleaned: Y / N	Oil Changed: Y / N	Maint. Needed: Y / N	

Keep track of how the foods process in your freeze-dryer.

Batch #		Start Cooling	Trays In	Trays Out	Run Time	Extra Dry	Total
		am pm	am pm	am pm	hrs	hrs	hrs
Start Date:		Customize / Temp / Time		Check Time:	am pm	am pm	am pm	
End Date:		Freeze / Dry		mTorr:				Subtract Dry from Wet for Water Loss
Tray Contents Description:	Examples: Raw, Cooked, Thickness, Liquid, Spread	Pre-Frozen	Wet grams	Check 1 grams	Check 2 grams	Dry grams	
1		Y / N					
2		Y / N					
3		Y / N					
4		Y / N					
Notes			Chamber Cleaned: Y / N	Oil Changed: Y / N	Maint. Needed: Y / N		

Batch #		Start Cooling	Trays In	Trays Out	Run Time	Extra Dry	Total
		am pm	am pm	am pm	hrs	hrs	hrs
Start Date:		Customize / Temp / Time		Check Time:	am pm	am pm	am pm	
End Date:		Freeze / Dry		mTorr:				Subtract Dry from Wet for Water Loss
Tray Contents Description:	Examples: Raw, Cooked, Thickness, Liquid, Spread	Pre-Frozen	Wet grams	Check 1 grams	Check 2 grams	Dry grams	
1		Y / N					
2		Y / N					
3		Y / N					
4		Y / N					
Notes			Chamber Cleaned: Y / N	Oil Changed: Y / N	Maint. Needed: Y / N		

Batch #		Start Cooling	Trays In	Trays Out	Run Time	Extra Dry	Total
		am pm	am pm	am pm	hrs	hrs	hrs
Start Date:		Customize / Temp / Time		Check Time:	am pm	am pm	am pm	
End Date:		Freeze / Dry		mTorr:				Subtract Dry from Wet for Water Loss
Tray Contents Description:	Examples: Raw, Cooked, Thickness, Liquid, Spread	Pre-Frozen	Wet grams	Check 1 grams	Check 2 grams	Dry grams	
1		Y / N					
2		Y / N					
3		Y / N					
4		Y / N					
Notes			Chamber Cleaned: Y / N	Oil Changed: Y / N	Maint. Needed: Y / N		

Keep track of how the foods process in your freeze-dryer.

Batch #		Start Cooling	Trays In	Trays Out	Run Time	Extra Dry	Total
		am pm	am pm	am pm	hrs	hrs	hrs
Start Date:		Customize	Temp	Time	Check Time:	am pm	am pm	am pm	
End Date:		Freeze							Subtract Dry from Wet for Water Loss
		Dry			mTorr:				
Tray Contents Description:	Examples: Raw, Cooked, Thickness, Liquid, Spread		Pre-Frozen	Wet grams	Check 1 grams	Check 2 grams	Dry grams	
1			Y / N					
2			Y / N					
3			Y / N					
4			Y / N					
Notes				Chamber Cleaned: Y / N	Oil Changed: Y / N	Maint. Needed: Y / N		

Batch #		Start Cooling	Trays In	Trays Out	Run Time	Extra Dry	Total
		am pm	am pm	am pm	hrs	hrs	hrs
Start Date:		Customize	Temp	Time	Check Time:	am pm	am pm	am pm	
End Date:		Freeze							Subtract Dry from Wet for Water Loss
		Dry			mTorr:				
Tray Contents Description:	Examples: Raw, Cooked, Thickness, Liquid, Spread		Pre-Frozen	Wet grams	Check 1 grams	Check 2 grams	Dry grams	
1			Y / N					
2			Y / N					
3			Y / N					
4			Y / N					
Notes				Chamber Cleaned: Y / N	Oil Changed: Y / N	Maint. Needed: Y / N		

Batch #		Start Cooling	Trays In	Trays Out	Run Time	Extra Dry	Total
		am pm	am pm	am pm	hrs	hrs	hrs
Start Date:		Customize	Temp	Time	Check Time:	am pm	am pm	am pm	
End Date:		Freeze							Subtract Dry from Wet for Water Loss
		Dry			mTorr:				
Tray Contents Description:	Examples: Raw, Cooked, Thickness, Liquid, Spread		Pre-Frozen	Wet grams	Check 1 grams	Check 2 grams	Dry grams	
1			Y / N					
2			Y / N					
3			Y / N					
4			Y / N					
Notes				Chamber Cleaned: Y / N	Oil Changed: Y / N	Maint. Needed: Y / N		

Keep track of how the foods process in your freeze-dryer.

Batch #		Start Cooling	Trays In	Trays Out	Run Time	Extra Dry	Total
		am / pm	am / pm	am / pm	hrs	hrs	hrs
Start Date:		Customize Temp Time		Check Time:	am / pm	am / pm	am / pm
End Date:		Freeze					Subtract Dry from Wet for Water Loss
		Dry		mTorr:			
Tray Contents Description:	Examples: Raw, Cooked, Thickness, Liquid, Spread		Pre-Frozen	Wet grams	Check 1 grams	Check 2 grams	Dry grams	
1			Y / N					
2			Y / N					
3			Y / N					
4			Y / N					
Notes				Chamber Cleaned: Y / N	Oil Changed: Y / N	Maint. Needed: Y / N	

Batch #		Start Cooling	Trays In	Trays Out	Run Time	Extra Dry	Total
		am / pm	am / pm	am / pm	hrs	hrs	hrs
Start Date:		Customize Temp Time		Check Time:	am / pm	am / pm	am / pm
End Date:		Freeze					Subtract Dry from Wet for Water Loss
		Dry		mTorr:			
Tray Contents Description:	Examples: Raw, Cooked, Thickness, Liquid, Spread		Pre-Frozen	Wet grams	Check 1 grams	Check 2 grams	Dry grams	
1			Y / N					
2			Y / N					
3			Y / N					
4			Y / N					
Notes				Chamber Cleaned: Y / N	Oil Changed: Y / N	Maint. Needed: Y / N	

Batch #		Start Cooling	Trays In	Trays Out	Run Time	Extra Dry	Total
		am / pm	am / pm	am / pm	hrs	hrs	hrs
Start Date:		Customize Temp Time		Check Time:	am / pm	am / pm	am / pm
End Date:		Freeze					Subtract Dry from Wet for Water Loss
		Dry		mTorr:			
Tray Contents Description:	Examples: Raw, Cooked, Thickness, Liquid, Spread		Pre-Frozen	Wet grams	Check 1 grams	Check 2 grams	Dry grams	
1			Y / N					
2			Y / N					
3			Y / N					
4			Y / N					
Notes				Chamber Cleaned: Y / N	Oil Changed: Y / N	Maint. Needed: Y / N	

Keep track of how the foods process in your freeze-dryer.

Batch #		Start Cooling	Trays In	Trays Out	Run Time	Extra Dry	Total
		am pm	am pm	am pm	hrs	hrs	hrs
Start Date:		Customize	Temp	Time	Check Time:	am pm	am pm	am pm	
End Date:		Freeze Dry			mTorr:				Subtract Dry from Wet for Water Loss
Tray Contents Description:	Examples: Raw, Cooked, Thickness, Liquid, Spread		Pre-Frozen	Wet grams	Check 1 grams	Check 2 grams	Dry grams	
1			Y / N					
2			Y / N					
3			Y / N					
4			Y / N					
Notes				Chamber Cleaned: Y / N	Oil Changed: Y / N	Maint. Needed: Y / N	

Batch #		Start Cooling	Trays In	Trays Out	Run Time	Extra Dry	Total
		am pm	am pm	am pm	hrs	hrs	hrs
Start Date:		Customize	Temp	Time	Check Time:	am pm	am pm	am pm	
End Date:		Freeze Dry			mTorr:				Subtract Dry from Wet for Water Loss
Tray Contents Description:	Examples: Raw, Cooked, Thickness, Liquid, Spread		Pre-Frozen	Wet grams	Check 1 grams	Check 2 grams	Dry grams	
1			Y / N					
2			Y / N					
3			Y / N					
4			Y / N					
Notes				Chamber Cleaned: Y / N	Oil Changed: Y / N	Maint. Needed: Y / N	

Batch #		Start Cooling	Trays In	Trays Out	Run Time	Extra Dry	Total
		am pm	am pm	am pm	hrs	hrs	hrs
Start Date:		Customize	Temp	Time	Check Time:	am pm	am pm	am pm	
End Date:		Freeze Dry			mTorr:				Subtract Dry from Wet for Water Loss
Tray Contents Description:	Examples: Raw, Cooked, Thickness, Liquid, Spread		Pre-Frozen	Wet grams	Check 1 grams	Check 2 grams	Dry grams	
1			Y / N					
2			Y / N					
3			Y / N					
4			Y / N					
Notes				Chamber Cleaned: Y / N	Oil Changed: Y / N	Maint. Needed: Y / N	

Keep track of how the foods process in your freeze-dryer.

Batch #		Start Cooling	Trays In	Trays Out	Run Time	Extra Dry	Total
		am / pm	am / pm	am / pm	hrs	hrs	hrs
Start Date:		Customize	Temp	Time	Check Time:	am / pm	am / pm	am / pm	Subtract Dry from Wet for Water Loss
End Date:		Freeze / Dry			mTorr:				
Tray Contents Description:	Examples: Raw, Cooked, Thickness, Liquid, Spread	Pre-Frozen	Wet grams	Check 1 grams	Check 2 grams	Dry grams	
1		Y / N					
2		Y / N					
3		Y / N					
4		Y / N					
Notes			Chamber Cleaned: Y / N	Oil Changed: Y / N	Maint. Needed: Y / N		

Batch #		Start Cooling	Trays In	Trays Out	Run Time	Extra Dry	Total
		am / pm	am / pm	am / pm	hrs	hrs	hrs
Start Date:		Customize	Temp	Time	Check Time:	am / pm	am / pm	am / pm	Subtract Dry from Wet for Water Loss
End Date:		Freeze / Dry			mTorr:				
Tray Contents Description:	Examples: Raw, Cooked, Thickness, Liquid, Spread	Pre-Frozen	Wet grams	Check 1 grams	Check 2 grams	Dry grams	
1		Y / N					
2		Y / N					
3		Y / N					
4		Y / N					
Notes			Chamber Cleaned: Y / N	Oil Changed: Y / N	Maint. Needed: Y / N		

Batch #		Start Cooling	Trays In	Trays Out	Run Time	Extra Dry	Total
		am / pm	am / pm	am / pm	hrs	hrs	hrs
Start Date:		Customize	Temp	Time	Check Time:	am / pm	am / pm	am / pm	Subtract Dry from Wet for Water Loss
End Date:		Freeze / Dry			mTorr:				
Tray Contents Description:	Examples: Raw, Cooked, Thickness, Liquid, Spread	Pre-Frozen	Wet grams	Check 1 grams	Check 2 grams	Dry grams	
1		Y / N					
2		Y / N					
3		Y / N					
4		Y / N					
Notes			Chamber Cleaned: Y / N	Oil Changed: Y / N	Maint. Needed: Y / N		

M   FREEZE-DRYER BATCH LOGS   PAGE#

Keep track of how the foods process in your freeze-dryer.

Batch #		Start Cooling	Trays In	Trays Out	Run Time	Extra Dry	Total
		am pm	am pm	am pm	hrs	hrs	hrs
Start Date:		Customize Temp	Time	Check Time:	am pm	am pm	am pm
		Freeze					
End Date:		Dry		mTorr:			Subtract Dry from Wet for Water Loss
Tray Contents Description:	Examples: Raw, Cooked, Thickness, Liquid, Spread	Pre-Frozen	Wet grams	Check 1 grams	Check 2 grams	Dry grams	
1		Y / N					
2		Y / N					
3		Y / N					
4		Y / N					
Notes			Chamber Cleaned: Y / N	Oil Changed: Y / N	Maint. Needed: Y / N		

Batch #		Start Cooling	Trays In	Trays Out	Run Time	Extra Dry	Total
		am pm	am pm	am pm	hrs	hrs	hrs
Start Date:		Customize Temp	Time	Check Time:	am pm	am pm	am pm
		Freeze					
End Date:		Dry		mTorr:			Subtract Dry from Wet for Water Loss
Tray Contents Description:	Examples: Raw, Cooked, Thickness, Liquid, Spread	Pre-Frozen	Wet grams	Check 1 grams	Check 2 grams	Dry grams	
1		Y / N					
2		Y / N					
3		Y / N					
4		Y / N					
Notes			Chamber Cleaned: Y / N	Oil Changed: Y / N	Maint. Needed: Y / N		

Batch #		Start Cooling	Trays In	Trays Out	Run Time	Extra Dry	Total
		am pm	am pm	am pm	hrs	hrs	hrs
Start Date:		Customize Temp	Time	Check Time:	am pm	am pm	am pm
		Freeze					
End Date:		Dry		mTorr:			Subtract Dry from Wet for Water Loss
Tray Contents Description:	Examples: Raw, Cooked, Thickness, Liquid, Spread	Pre-Frozen	Wet grams	Check 1 grams	Check 2 grams	Dry grams	
1		Y / N					
2		Y / N					
3		Y / N					
4		Y / N					
Notes			Chamber Cleaned: Y / N	Oil Changed: Y / N	Maint. Needed: Y / N		

Keep track of how the foods process in your freeze-dryer.

Batch #		Start Cooling	Trays In	Trays Out	Run Time	Extra Dry	Total
		am pm	am pm	am pm	hrs	hrs	hrs
Start Date:		Customize	Temp	Time	Check Time:	am pm	am pm	am pm	
End Date:		Freeze Dry			mTorr:				Subtract Dry from Wet for Water Loss
Tray Contents Description:	Examples: Raw, Cooked, Thickness, Liquid, Spread		Pre-Frozen	Wet grams	Check 1 grams	Check 2 grams	Dry grams	
1			Y / N					
2			Y / N					
3			Y / N					
4			Y / N					
Notes				Chamber Cleaned: Y / N	Oil Changed: Y / N	Maint. Needed: Y / N	

Batch #		Start Cooling	Trays In	Trays Out	Run Time	Extra Dry	Total
		am pm	am pm	am pm	hrs	hrs	hrs
Start Date:		Customize	Temp	Time	Check Time:	am pm	am pm	am pm	
End Date:		Freeze Dry			mTorr:				Subtract Dry from Wet for Water Loss
Tray Contents Description:	Examples: Raw, Cooked, Thickness, Liquid, Spread		Pre-Frozen	Wet grams	Check 1 grams	Check 2 grams	Dry grams	
1			Y / N					
2			Y / N					
3			Y / N					
4			Y / N					
Notes				Chamber Cleaned: Y / N	Oil Changed: Y / N	Maint. Needed: Y / N	

Batch #		Start Cooling	Trays In	Trays Out	Run Time	Extra Dry	Total
		am pm	am pm	am pm	hrs	hrs	hrs
Start Date:		Customize	Temp	Time	Check Time:	am pm	am pm	am pm	
End Date:		Freeze Dry			mTorr:				Subtract Dry from Wet for Water Loss
Tray Contents Description:	Examples: Raw, Cooked, Thickness, Liquid, Spread		Pre-Frozen	Wet grams	Check 1 grams	Check 2 grams	Dry grams	
1			Y / N					
2			Y / N					
3			Y / N					
4			Y / N					
Notes				Chamber Cleaned: Y / N	Oil Changed: Y / N	Maint. Needed: Y / N	

M   FREEZE-DRYER BATCH LOGS   PAGE#

Keep track of how the foods process in your freeze-dryer.

Batch #		Start Cooling	Trays In	Trays Out	Run Time	Extra Dry	Total
		am pm	am pm	am pm	hrs	hrs	hrs
Start Date:		Customize Temp Time		Check Time:	am pm	am pm	am pm	Subtract Dry from Wet for Water Loss
End Date:		Freeze / Dry		mTorr:				
Tray Contents Description:	Examples: Raw, Cooked, Thickness, Liquid, Spread	Pre-Frozen	Wet grams	Check 1 grams	Check 2 grams	Dry grams	
1		Y / N					
2		Y / N					
3		Y / N					
4		Y / N					
Notes			Chamber Cleaned: Y / N	Oil Changed: Y / N	Maint. Needed: Y / N		

Batch #		Start Cooling	Trays In	Trays Out	Run Time	Extra Dry	Total
		am pm	am pm	am pm	hrs	hrs	hrs
Start Date:		Customize Temp Time		Check Time:	am pm	am pm	am pm	Subtract Dry from Wet for Water Loss
End Date:		Freeze / Dry		mTorr:				
Tray Contents Description:	Examples: Raw, Cooked, Thickness, Liquid, Spread	Pre-Frozen	Wet grams	Check 1 grams	Check 2 grams	Dry grams	
1		Y / N					
2		Y / N					
3		Y / N					
4		Y / N					
Notes			Chamber Cleaned: Y / N	Oil Changed: Y / N	Maint. Needed: Y / N		

Batch #		Start Cooling	Trays In	Trays Out	Run Time	Extra Dry	Total
		am pm	am pm	am pm	hrs	hrs	hrs
Start Date:		Customize Temp Time		Check Time:	am pm	am pm	am pm	Subtract Dry from Wet for Water Loss
End Date:		Freeze / Dry		mTorr:				
Tray Contents Description:	Examples: Raw, Cooked, Thickness, Liquid, Spread	Pre-Frozen	Wet grams	Check 1 grams	Check 2 grams	Dry grams	
1		Y / N					
2		Y / N					
3		Y / N					
4		Y / N					
Notes			Chamber Cleaned: Y / N	Oil Changed: Y / N	Maint. Needed: Y / N		

Keep track of how the foods process in your freeze-dryer.

Batch #		Start Cooling	Trays In	Trays Out	Run Time	Extra Dry	Total
		am / pm	am / pm	am / pm	hrs	hrs	hrs
Start Date:		Customize Temp Time		Check Time:	am / pm	am / pm	am / pm
End Date:		Freeze					Subtract Dry from Wet for Water Loss
		Dry		mTorr:			
Tray Contents Description:	Examples: Raw, Cooked, Thickness, Liquid, Spread		Pre-Frozen	Wet grams	Check 1 grams	Check 2 grams	Dry grams
1			Y / N				
2			Y / N				
3			Y / N				
4			Y / N				
Notes				Chamber Cleaned: Y / N	Oil Changed: Y / N	Maint. Needed: Y / N	

Batch #		Start Cooling	Trays In	Trays Out	Run Time	Extra Dry	Total
		am / pm	am / pm	am / pm	hrs	hrs	hrs
Start Date:		Customize Temp Time		Check Time:	am / pm	am / pm	am / pm
End Date:		Freeze					Subtract Dry from Wet for Water Loss
		Dry		mTorr:			
Tray Contents Description:	Examples: Raw, Cooked, Thickness, Liquid, Spread		Pre-Frozen	Wet grams	Check 1 grams	Check 2 grams	Dry grams
1			Y / N				
2			Y / N				
3			Y / N				
4			Y / N				
Notes				Chamber Cleaned: Y / N	Oil Changed: Y / N	Maint. Needed: Y / N	

Batch #		Start Cooling	Trays In	Trays Out	Run Time	Extra Dry	Total
		am / pm	am / pm	am / pm	hrs	hrs	hrs
Start Date:		Customize Temp Time		Check Time:	am / pm	am / pm	am / pm
End Date:		Freeze					Subtract Dry from Wet for Water Loss
		Dry		mTorr:			
Tray Contents Description:	Examples: Raw, Cooked, Thickness, Liquid, Spread		Pre-Frozen	Wet grams	Check 1 grams	Check 2 grams	Dry grams
1			Y / N				
2			Y / N				
3			Y / N				
4			Y / N				
Notes				Chamber Cleaned: Y / N	Oil Changed: Y / N	Maint. Needed: Y / N	

M   FREEZE-DRYER BATCH LOGS   PAGE#

Keep track of how the foods process in your freeze-dryer.

Batch #		Start Cooling	Trays In	Trays Out	Run Time	Extra Dry	Total
		am pm	am pm	am pm	hrs	hrs	hrs
Start Date:		Customize Temp	Time	Check Time:	am pm	am pm	am pm
End Date:		Freeze						Subtract Dry from Wet for Water Loss
		Dry		mTorr:			
Tray Contents Description:	Examples: Raw, Cooked, Thickness, Liquid, Spread		Pre-Frozen	Wet grams	Check 1 grams	Check 2 grams	Dry grams	
1			Y / N					
2			Y / N					
3			Y / N					
4			Y / N					
Notes				Chamber Cleaned: Y / N	Oil Changed: Y / N	Maint. Needed: Y / N	

Batch #		Start Cooling	Trays In	Trays Out	Run Time	Extra Dry	Total
		am pm	am pm	am pm	hrs	hrs	hrs
Start Date:		Customize Temp	Time	Check Time:	am pm	am pm	am pm
End Date:		Freeze						Subtract Dry from Wet for Water Loss
		Dry		mTorr:			
Tray Contents Description:	Examples: Raw, Cooked, Thickness, Liquid, Spread		Pre-Frozen	Wet grams	Check 1 grams	Check 2 grams	Dry grams	
1			Y / N					
2			Y / N					
3			Y / N					
4			Y / N					
Notes				Chamber Cleaned: Y / N	Oil Changed: Y / N	Maint. Needed: Y / N	

Batch #		Start Cooling	Trays In	Trays Out	Run Time	Extra Dry	Total
		am pm	am pm	am pm	hrs	hrs	hrs
Start Date:		Customize Temp	Time	Check Time:	am pm	am pm	am pm
End Date:		Freeze						Subtract Dry from Wet for Water Loss
		Dry		mTorr:			
Tray Contents Description:	Examples: Raw, Cooked, Thickness, Liquid, Spread		Pre-Frozen	Wet grams	Check 1 grams	Check 2 grams	Dry grams	
1			Y / N					
2			Y / N					
3			Y / N					
4			Y / N					
Notes				Chamber Cleaned: Y / N	Oil Changed: Y / N	Maint. Needed: Y / N	

Keep track of how the foods process in your freeze-dryer.

Batch #		Start Cooling	Trays In	Trays Out	Run Time	Extra Dry	Total
		am pm	am pm	am pm	hrs	hrs	hrs
Start Date:		Customize Temp Time		Check Time:	am pm	am pm	am pm	Subtract Dry from Wet for Water Loss
End Date:		Freeze						
		Dry		mTorr:				
Tray Contents Description:	Examples: Raw, Cooked, Thickness, Liquid, Spread	Pre-Frozen	Wet grams	Check 1 grams	Check 2 grams	Dry grams	
1		Y / N					
2		Y / N					
3		Y / N					
4		Y / N					
Notes			Chamber Cleaned: Y / N	Oil Changed: Y / N	Maint. Needed: Y / N		

Batch #		Start Cooling	Trays In	Trays Out	Run Time	Extra Dry	Total
		am pm	am pm	am pm	hrs	hrs	hrs
Start Date:		Customize Temp Time		Check Time:	am pm	am pm	am pm	Subtract Dry from Wet for Water Loss
End Date:		Freeze						
		Dry		mTorr:				
Tray Contents Description:	Examples: Raw, Cooked, Thickness, Liquid, Spread	Pre-Frozen	Wet grams	Check 1 grams	Check 2 grams	Dry grams	
1		Y / N					
2		Y / N					
3		Y / N					
4		Y / N					
Notes			Chamber Cleaned: Y / N	Oil Changed: Y / N	Maint. Needed: Y / N		

Batch #		Start Cooling	Trays In	Trays Out	Run Time	Extra Dry	Total
		am pm	am pm	am pm	hrs	hrs	hrs
Start Date:		Customize Temp Time		Check Time:	am pm	am pm	am pm	Subtract Dry from Wet for Water Loss
End Date:		Freeze						
		Dry		mTorr:				
Tray Contents Description:	Examples: Raw, Cooked, Thickness, Liquid, Spread	Pre-Frozen	Wet grams	Check 1 grams	Check 2 grams	Dry grams	
1		Y / N					
2		Y / N					
3		Y / N					
4		Y / N					
Notes			Chamber Cleaned: Y / N	Oil Changed: Y / N	Maint. Needed: Y / N		

Keep track of how the foods process in your freeze-dryer.

Batch #		Start Cooling	Trays In	Trays Out	Run Time	Extra Dry	Total
		am pm	am pm	am pm	hrs	hrs	hrs
Start Date:		Customize	Temp	Time	Check Time:	am pm	am pm	am pm	Subtract Dry from Wet for Water Loss
End Date:		Freeze							
		Dry			mTorr:				
Tray Contents Description:	Examples: Raw, Cooked, Thickness, Liquid, Spread		Pre-Frozen	Wet grams	Check 1 grams	Check 2 grams	Dry grams	
1			Y / N					
2			Y / N					
3			Y / N					
4			Y / N					
Notes				Chamber Cleaned: Y / N	Oil Changed: Y / N	Maint. Needed: Y / N	

Batch #		Start Cooling	Trays In	Trays Out	Run Time	Extra Dry	Total
		am pm	am pm	am pm	hrs	hrs	hrs
Start Date:		Customize	Temp	Time	Check Time:	am pm	am pm	am pm	Subtract Dry from Wet for Water Loss
End Date:		Freeze							
		Dry			mTorr:				
Tray Contents Description:	Examples: Raw, Cooked, Thickness, Liquid, Spread		Pre-Frozen	Wet grams	Check 1 grams	Check 2 grams	Dry grams	
1			Y / N					
2			Y / N					
3			Y / N					
4			Y / N					
Notes				Chamber Cleaned: Y / N	Oil Changed: Y / N	Maint. Needed: Y / N	

Batch #		Start Cooling	Trays In	Trays Out	Run Time	Extra Dry	Total
		am pm	am pm	am pm	hrs	hrs	hrs
Start Date:		Customize	Temp	Time	Check Time:	am pm	am pm	am pm	Subtract Dry from Wet for Water Loss
End Date:		Freeze							
		Dry			mTorr:				
Tray Contents Description:	Examples: Raw, Cooked, Thickness, Liquid, Spread		Pre-Frozen	Wet grams	Check 1 grams	Check 2 grams	Dry grams	
1			Y / N					
2			Y / N					
3			Y / N					
4			Y / N					
Notes				Chamber Cleaned: Y / N	Oil Changed: Y / N	Maint. Needed: Y / N	

Keep track of how the foods process in your freeze-dryer.

Batch #		Start Cooling	Trays In	Trays Out	Run Time	Extra Dry	Total
		am pm	am pm	am pm	hrs	hrs	hrs
Start Date:		Customize Temp Time		Check Time:	am pm	am pm	am pm	Subtract Dry from Wet for Water Loss
End Date:		Freeze / Dry		mTorr:				
Tray Contents Description:	Examples: Raw, Cooked, Thickness, Liquid, Spread	Pre-Frozen	Wet grams	Check 1 grams	Check 2 grams	Dry grams	
1		Y / N					
2		Y / N					
3		Y / N					
4		Y / N					
Notes			Chamber Cleaned: Y / N	Oil Changed: Y / N	Maint. Needed: Y / N		

Batch #		Start Cooling	Trays In	Trays Out	Run Time	Extra Dry	Total
		am pm	am pm	am pm	hrs	hrs	hrs
Start Date:		Customize Temp Time		Check Time:	am pm	am pm	am pm	Subtract Dry from Wet for Water Loss
End Date:		Freeze / Dry		mTorr:				
Tray Contents Description:	Examples: Raw, Cooked, Thickness, Liquid, Spread	Pre-Frozen	Wet grams	Check 1 grams	Check 2 grams	Dry grams	
1		Y / N					
2		Y / N					
3		Y / N					
4		Y / N					
Notes			Chamber Cleaned: Y / N	Oil Changed: Y / N	Maint. Needed: Y / N		

Batch #		Start Cooling	Trays In	Trays Out	Run Time	Extra Dry	Total
		am pm	am pm	am pm	hrs	hrs	hrs
Start Date:		Customize Temp Time		Check Time:	am pm	am pm	am pm	Subtract Dry from Wet for Water Loss
End Date:		Freeze / Dry		mTorr:				
Tray Contents Description:	Examples: Raw, Cooked, Thickness, Liquid, Spread	Pre-Frozen	Wet grams	Check 1 grams	Check 2 grams	Dry grams	
1		Y / N					
2		Y / N					
3		Y / N					
4		Y / N					
Notes			Chamber Cleaned: Y / N	Oil Changed: Y / N	Maint. Needed: Y / N		

M   FREEZE-DRYER BATCH LOGS

Keep track of how the foods process in your freeze-dryer.

Batch #		Start Cooling	Trays In	Trays Out	Run Time	Extra Dry	Total
		am pm	am pm	am pm	hrs	hrs	hrs
Start Date:		Customize Temp	Time	Check Time:	am pm	am pm	am pm
End Date:		Freeze / Dry		mTorr:			Subtract Dry from Wet for Water Loss
Tray Contents Description:	Examples: Raw, Cooked, Thickness, Liquid, Spread	Pre-Frozen	Wet grams	Check 1 grams	Check 2 grams	Dry grams	
1		Y / N					
2		Y / N					
3		Y / N					
4		Y / N					
Notes			Chamber Cleaned: Y / N	Oil Changed: Y / N	Maint. Needed: Y / N		

Batch #		Start Cooling	Trays In	Trays Out	Run Time	Extra Dry	Total
		am pm	am pm	am pm	hrs	hrs	hrs
Start Date:		Customize Temp	Time	Check Time:	am pm	am pm	am pm
End Date:		Freeze / Dry		mTorr:			Subtract Dry from Wet for Water Loss
Tray Contents Description:	Examples: Raw, Cooked, Thickness, Liquid, Spread	Pre-Frozen	Wet grams	Check 1 grams	Check 2 grams	Dry grams	
1		Y / N					
2		Y / N					
3		Y / N					
4		Y / N					
Notes			Chamber Cleaned: Y / N	Oil Changed: Y / N	Maint. Needed: Y / N		

Batch #		Start Cooling	Trays In	Trays Out	Run Time	Extra Dry	Total
		am pm	am pm	am pm	hrs	hrs	hrs
Start Date:		Customize Temp	Time	Check Time:	am pm	am pm	am pm
End Date:		Freeze / Dry		mTorr:			Subtract Dry from Wet for Water Loss
Tray Contents Description:	Examples: Raw, Cooked, Thickness, Liquid, Spread	Pre-Frozen	Wet grams	Check 1 grams	Check 2 grams	Dry grams	
1		Y / N					
2		Y / N					
3		Y / N					
4		Y / N					
Notes			Chamber Cleaned: Y / N	Oil Changed: Y / N	Maint. Needed: Y / N		

Keep track of how the foods process in your freeze-dryer.

Batch #		Start Cooling	Trays In	Trays Out	Run Time	Extra Dry	Total
		am pm	am pm	am pm	hrs	hrs	hrs
Start Date:		Customize	Temp	Time	Check Time:	am pm	am pm	am pm	
End Date:		Freeze Dry			mTorr:				Subtract Dry from Wet for Water Loss
Tray Contents Description:	Examples: Raw, Cooked, Thickness, Liquid, Spread		Pre-Frozen	Wet grams	Check 1 grams	Check 2 grams	Dry grams	
1			Y / N					
2			Y / N					
3			Y / N					
4			Y / N					
Notes				Chamber Cleaned: Y / N	Oil Changed: Y / N	Maint. Needed: Y / N	

Batch #		Start Cooling	Trays In	Trays Out	Run Time	Extra Dry	Total
		am pm	am pm	am pm	hrs	hrs	hrs
Start Date:		Customize	Temp	Time	Check Time:	am pm	am pm	am pm	
End Date:		Freeze Dry			mTorr:				Subtract Dry from Wet for Water Loss
Tray Contents Description:	Examples: Raw, Cooked, Thickness, Liquid, Spread		Pre-Frozen	Wet grams	Check 1 grams	Check 2 grams	Dry grams	
1			Y / N					
2			Y / N					
3			Y / N					
4			Y / N					
Notes				Chamber Cleaned: Y / N	Oil Changed: Y / N	Maint. Needed: Y / N	

Batch #		Start Cooling	Trays In	Trays Out	Run Time	Extra Dry	Total
		am pm	am pm	am pm	hrs	hrs	hrs
Start Date:		Customize	Temp	Time	Check Time:	am pm	am pm	am pm	
End Date:		Freeze Dry			mTorr:				Subtract Dry from Wet for Water Loss
Tray Contents Description:	Examples: Raw, Cooked, Thickness, Liquid, Spread		Pre-Frozen	Wet grams	Check 1 grams	Check 2 grams	Dry grams	
1			Y / N					
2			Y / N					
3			Y / N					
4			Y / N					
Notes				Chamber Cleaned: Y / N	Oil Changed: Y / N	Maint. Needed: Y / N	

Keep track of how the foods process in your freeze-dryer.

Batch #		Start Cooling	Trays In	Trays Out	Run Time	Extra Dry	Total
		am pm	am pm	am pm	hrs	hrs	hrs
Start Date:		Customize Temp	Time	Check Time:	am pm	am pm	am pm
End Date:		Freeze					Subtract Dry from Wet for Water Loss
		Dry		mTorr:			
Tray Contents Description:	Examples: Raw, Cooked, Thickness, Liquid, Spread		Pre-Frozen	Wet grams	Check 1 grams	Check 2 grams	Dry grams
1			Y / N				
2			Y / N				
3			Y / N				
4			Y / N				
Notes				Chamber Cleaned: Y / N	Oil Changed: Y / N	Maint. Needed: Y / N	

Batch #		Start Cooling	Trays In	Trays Out	Run Time	Extra Dry	Total
		am pm	am pm	am pm	hrs	hrs	hrs
Start Date:		Customize Temp	Time	Check Time:	am pm	am pm	am pm
End Date:		Freeze					Subtract Dry from Wet for Water Loss
		Dry		mTorr:			
Tray Contents Description:	Examples: Raw, Cooked, Thickness, Liquid, Spread		Pre-Frozen	Wet grams	Check 1 grams	Check 2 grams	Dry grams
1			Y / N				
2			Y / N				
3			Y / N				
4			Y / N				
Notes				Chamber Cleaned: Y / N	Oil Changed: Y / N	Maint. Needed: Y / N	

Batch #		Start Cooling	Trays In	Trays Out	Run Time	Extra Dry	Total
		am pm	am pm	am pm	hrs	hrs	hrs
Start Date:		Customize Temp	Time	Check Time:	am pm	am pm	am pm
End Date:		Freeze					Subtract Dry from Wet for Water Loss
		Dry		mTorr:			
Tray Contents Description:	Examples: Raw, Cooked, Thickness, Liquid, Spread		Pre-Frozen	Wet grams	Check 1 grams	Check 2 grams	Dry grams
1			Y / N				
2			Y / N				
3			Y / N				
4			Y / N				
Notes				Chamber Cleaned: Y / N	Oil Changed: Y / N	Maint. Needed: Y / N	

Keep track of how the foods process in your freeze-dryer.

Batch #		Start Cooling	Trays In	Trays Out	Run Time	Extra Dry	Total
		am pm	am pm	am pm	hrs	hrs	hrs
Start Date:		Customize Temp	Time	Check Time:	am pm	am pm	am pm
End Date:		Freeze Dry		mTorr:			Subtract Dry from Wet for Water Loss
Tray Contents Description:	Examples: Raw, Cooked, Thickness, Liquid, Spread		Pre-Frozen	Wet grams	Check 1 grams	Check 2 grams	Dry grams	
1			Y / N					
2			Y / N					
3			Y / N					
4			Y / N					
Notes				Chamber Cleaned: Y / N	Oil Changed: Y / N	Maint. Needed: Y / N	

Batch #		Start Cooling	Trays In	Trays Out	Run Time	Extra Dry	Total
		am pm	am pm	am pm	hrs	hrs	hrs
Start Date:		Customize Temp	Time	Check Time:	am pm	am pm	am pm
End Date:		Freeze Dry		mTorr:			Subtract Dry from Wet for Water Loss
Tray Contents Description:	Examples: Raw, Cooked, Thickness, Liquid, Spread		Pre-Frozen	Wet grams	Check 1 grams	Check 2 grams	Dry grams	
1			Y / N					
2			Y / N					
3			Y / N					
4			Y / N					
Notes				Chamber Cleaned: Y / N	Oil Changed: Y / N	Maint. Needed: Y / N	

Batch #		Start Cooling	Trays In	Trays Out	Run Time	Extra Dry	Total
		am pm	am pm	am pm	hrs	hrs	hrs
Start Date:		Customize Temp	Time	Check Time:	am pm	am pm	am pm
End Date:		Freeze Dry		mTorr:			Subtract Dry from Wet for Water Loss
Tray Contents Description:	Examples: Raw, Cooked, Thickness, Liquid, Spread		Pre-Frozen	Wet grams	Check 1 grams	Check 2 grams	Dry grams	
1			Y / N					
2			Y / N					
3			Y / N					
4			Y / N					
Notes				Chamber Cleaned: Y / N	Oil Changed: Y / N	Maint. Needed: Y / N	

Keep track of how the foods process in your freeze-dryer.

Batch #		Start Cooling	Trays In	Trays Out	Run Time	Extra Dry	Total
		am pm	am pm	am pm	hrs	hrs	hrs
Start Date:		Customize	Temp	Time	Check Time:	am pm	am pm	am pm	
End Date:		Freeze							Subtract Dry from Wet for Water Loss
		Dry			mTorr:				
Tray Contents Description:	Examples: Raw, Cooked, Thickness, Liquid, Spread	Pre-Frozen	Wet grams	Check 1 grams	Check 2 grams	Dry grams	
1		Y / N					
2		Y / N					
3		Y / N					
4		Y / N					
Notes		Chamber Cleaned: Y / N	Oil Changed: Y / N	Maint. Needed: Y / N			

Batch #		Start Cooling	Trays In	Trays Out	Run Time	Extra Dry	Total
		am pm	am pm	am pm	hrs	hrs	hrs
Start Date:		Customize	Temp	Time	Check Time:	am pm	am pm	am pm	
End Date:		Freeze							Subtract Dry from Wet for Water Loss
		Dry			mTorr:				
Tray Contents Description:	Examples: Raw, Cooked, Thickness, Liquid, Spread	Pre-Frozen	Wet grams	Check 1 grams	Check 2 grams	Dry grams	
1		Y / N					
2		Y / N					
3		Y / N					
4		Y / N					
Notes		Chamber Cleaned: Y / N	Oil Changed: Y / N	Maint. Needed: Y / N			

Batch #		Start Cooling	Trays In	Trays Out	Run Time	Extra Dry	Total
		am pm	am pm	am pm	hrs	hrs	hrs
Start Date:		Customize	Temp	Time	Check Time:	am pm	am pm	am pm	
End Date:		Freeze							Subtract Dry from Wet for Water Loss
		Dry			mTorr:				
Tray Contents Description:	Examples: Raw, Cooked, Thickness, Liquid, Spread	Pre-Frozen	Wet grams	Check 1 grams	Check 2 grams	Dry grams	
1		Y / N					
2		Y / N					
3		Y / N					
4		Y / N					
Notes		Chamber Cleaned: Y / N	Oil Changed: Y / N	Maint. Needed: Y / N			

Keep track of how the foods process in your freeze-dryer.

Batch #		Start Cooling	Trays In	Trays Out	Run Time	Extra Dry	Total
		am pm	am pm	am pm	hrs	hrs	hrs
Start Date:		Customize / Temp / Time		Check Time:	am pm	am pm	am pm	Subtract Dry from Wet for Water Loss
End Date:		Freeze / Dry		mTorr:				

Tray Contents Description:	Examples: Raw, Cooked, Thickness, Liquid, Spread	Pre-Frozen	Wet grams	Check 1 grams	Check 2 grams	Dry grams	
1		Y / N					
2		Y / N					
3		Y / N					
4		Y / N					
Notes			Chamber Cleaned: Y / N	Oil Changed: Y / N	Maint. Needed: Y / N		

Batch #		Start Cooling	Trays In	Trays Out	Run Time	Extra Dry	Total
		am pm	am pm	am pm	hrs	hrs	hrs
Start Date:		Customize / Temp / Time		Check Time:	am pm	am pm	am pm	Subtract Dry from Wet for Water Loss
End Date:		Freeze / Dry		mTorr:				

Tray Contents Description:	Examples: Raw, Cooked, Thickness, Liquid, Spread	Pre-Frozen	Wet grams	Check 1 grams	Check 2 grams	Dry grams	
1		Y / N					
2		Y / N					
3		Y / N					
4		Y / N					
Notes			Chamber Cleaned: Y / N	Oil Changed: Y / N	Maint. Needed: Y / N		

Batch #		Start Cooling	Trays In	Trays Out	Run Time	Extra Dry	Total
		am pm	am pm	am pm	hrs	hrs	hrs
Start Date:		Customize / Temp / Time		Check Time:	am pm	am pm	am pm	Subtract Dry from Wet for Water Loss
End Date:		Freeze / Dry		mTorr:				

Tray Contents Description:	Examples: Raw, Cooked, Thickness, Liquid, Spread	Pre-Frozen	Wet grams	Check 1 grams	Check 2 grams	Dry grams	
1		Y / N					
2		Y / N					
3		Y / N					
4		Y / N					
Notes			Chamber Cleaned: Y / N	Oil Changed: Y / N	Maint. Needed: Y / N		

M FREEZE-DRYER BATCH LOGS

Keep track of how the foods process in your freeze-dryer.

Batch #		Start Cooling	Trays In	Trays Out	Run Time	Extra Dry	Total
		am pm	am pm	am pm	hrs	hrs	hrs
Start Date:		Customize Temp	Time	Check Time:	am pm	am pm	am pm
End Date:		Freeze					Subtract Dry from Wet for Water Loss
		Dry		mTorr:			
Tray Contents Description:	Examples: Raw, Cooked, Thickness, Liquid, Spread	Pre-Frozen	Wet grams	Check 1 grams	Check 2 grams	Dry grams	
1		Y / N					
2		Y / N					
3		Y / N					
4		Y / N					
Notes			Chamber Cleaned: Y / N	Oil Changed: Y / N	Maint. Needed: Y / N		

Batch #		Start Cooling	Trays In	Trays Out	Run Time	Extra Dry	Total
		am pm	am pm	am pm	hrs	hrs	hrs
Start Date:		Customize Temp	Time	Check Time:	am pm	am pm	am pm
End Date:		Freeze					Subtract Dry from Wet for Water Loss
		Dry		mTorr:			
Tray Contents Description:	Examples: Raw, Cooked, Thickness, Liquid, Spread	Pre-Frozen	Wet grams	Check 1 grams	Check 2 grams	Dry grams	
1		Y / N					
2		Y / N					
3		Y / N					
4		Y / N					
Notes			Chamber Cleaned: Y / N	Oil Changed: Y / N	Maint. Needed: Y / N		

Batch #		Start Cooling	Trays In	Trays Out	Run Time	Extra Dry	Total
		am pm	am pm	am pm	hrs	hrs	hrs
Start Date:		Customize Temp	Time	Check Time:	am pm	am pm	am pm
End Date:		Freeze					Subtract Dry from Wet for Water Loss
		Dry		mTorr:			
Tray Contents Description:	Examples: Raw, Cooked, Thickness, Liquid, Spread	Pre-Frozen	Wet grams	Check 1 grams	Check 2 grams	Dry grams	
1		Y / N					
2		Y / N					
3		Y / N					
4		Y / N					
Notes			Chamber Cleaned: Y / N	Oil Changed: Y / N	Maint. Needed: Y / N		

Keep track of how the foods process in your freeze-dryer.

Batch #		Start Cooling	Trays In	Trays Out	Run Time	Extra Dry	Total
		am pm	am pm	am pm	hrs	hrs	hrs
Start Date:		Customize	Temp	Time	Check Time:	am pm	am pm	am pm	
End Date:		Freeze / Dry			mTorr:				Subtract Dry from Wet for Water Loss
Tray Contents Description:	Examples: Raw, Cooked, Thickness, Liquid, Spread		Pre-Frozen	Wet grams	Check 1 grams	Check 2 grams	Dry grams	
1			Y / N					
2			Y / N					
3			Y / N					
4			Y / N					
Notes				Chamber Cleaned: Y / N	Oil Changed: Y / N	Maint. Needed: Y / N	

Batch #		Start Cooling	Trays In	Trays Out	Run Time	Extra Dry	Total
		am pm	am pm	am pm	hrs	hrs	hrs
Start Date:		Customize	Temp	Time	Check Time:	am pm	am pm	am pm	
End Date:		Freeze / Dry			mTorr:				Subtract Dry from Wet for Water Loss
Tray Contents Description:	Examples: Raw, Cooked, Thickness, Liquid, Spread		Pre-Frozen	Wet grams	Check 1 grams	Check 2 grams	Dry grams	
1			Y / N					
2			Y / N					
3			Y / N					
4			Y / N					
Notes				Chamber Cleaned: Y / N	Oil Changed: Y / N	Maint. Needed: Y / N	

Batch #		Start Cooling	Trays In	Trays Out	Run Time	Extra Dry	Total
		am pm	am pm	am pm	hrs	hrs	hrs
Start Date:		Customize	Temp	Time	Check Time:	am pm	am pm	am pm	
End Date:		Freeze / Dry			mTorr:				Subtract Dry from Wet for Water Loss
Tray Contents Description:	Examples: Raw, Cooked, Thickness, Liquid, Spread		Pre-Frozen	Wet grams	Check 1 grams	Check 2 grams	Dry grams	
1			Y / N					
2			Y / N					
3			Y / N					
4			Y / N					
Notes				Chamber Cleaned: Y / N	Oil Changed: Y / N	Maint. Needed: Y / N	

M   FREEZE-DRYER BATCH LOGS

Keep track of how the foods process in your freeze-dryer.

Batch #		Start Cooling	Trays In	Trays Out	Run Time	Extra Dry	Total
		am pm	am pm	am pm	hrs	hrs	hrs
Start Date:		Customize Temp	Time	Check Time:	am pm	am pm	am pm
End Date:		Freeze Dry		mTorr:			Subtract Dry from Wet for Water Loss
Tray Contents Description:	Examples: Raw, Cooked, Thickness, Liquid, Spread	Pre-Frozen	Wet grams	Check 1 grams	Check 2 grams	Dry grams	
1		Y / N					
2		Y / N					
3		Y / N					
4		Y / N					
Notes			Chamber Cleaned: Y / N	Oil Changed: Y / N	Maint. Needed: Y / N		

Batch #		Start Cooling	Trays In	Trays Out	Run Time	Extra Dry	Total
		am pm	am pm	am pm	hrs	hrs	hrs
Start Date:		Customize Temp	Time	Check Time:	am pm	am pm	am pm
End Date:		Freeze Dry		mTorr:			Subtract Dry from Wet for Water Loss
Tray Contents Description:	Examples: Raw, Cooked, Thickness, Liquid, Spread	Pre-Frozen	Wet grams	Check 1 grams	Check 2 grams	Dry grams	
1		Y / N					
2		Y / N					
3		Y / N					
4		Y / N					
Notes			Chamber Cleaned: Y / N	Oil Changed: Y / N	Maint. Needed: Y / N		

Batch #		Start Cooling	Trays In	Trays Out	Run Time	Extra Dry	Total
		am pm	am pm	am pm	hrs	hrs	hrs
Start Date:		Customize Temp	Time	Check Time:	am pm	am pm	am pm
End Date:		Freeze Dry		mTorr:			Subtract Dry from Wet for Water Loss
Tray Contents Description:	Examples: Raw, Cooked, Thickness, Liquid, Spread	Pre-Frozen	Wet grams	Check 1 grams	Check 2 grams	Dry grams	
1		Y / N					
2		Y / N					
3		Y / N					
4		Y / N					
Notes			Chamber Cleaned: Y / N	Oil Changed: Y / N	Maint. Needed: Y / N		

M   FREEZE-DRYER BATCH LOGS   PAGE#

Keep track of how the foods process in your freeze-dryer.

Batch #		Start Cooling	Trays In	Trays Out	Run Time	Extra Dry	Total
		am pm	am pm	am pm	hrs	hrs	hrs
Start Date:		Customize Temp	Time	Check Time:	am pm	am pm	am pm
End Date:		Freeze / Dry		mTorr:			Subtract Dry from Wet for Water Loss
Tray Contents Description:	Examples: Raw, Cooked, Thickness, Liquid, Spread		Pre-Frozen	Wet grams	Check 1 grams	Check 2 grams	Dry grams
1			Y / N				
2			Y / N				
3			Y / N				
4			Y / N				
Notes			Chamber Cleaned: Y / N	Oil Changed: Y / N	Maint. Needed: Y / N		

Batch #		Start Cooling	Trays In	Trays Out	Run Time	Extra Dry	Total
		am pm	am pm	am pm	hrs	hrs	hrs
Start Date:		Customize Temp	Time	Check Time:	am pm	am pm	am pm
End Date:		Freeze / Dry		mTorr:			Subtract Dry from Wet for Water Loss
Tray Contents Description:	Examples: Raw, Cooked, Thickness, Liquid, Spread		Pre-Frozen	Wet grams	Check 1 grams	Check 2 grams	Dry grams
1			Y / N				
2			Y / N				
3			Y / N				
4			Y / N				
Notes			Chamber Cleaned: Y / N	Oil Changed: Y / N	Maint. Needed: Y / N		

Batch #		Start Cooling	Trays In	Trays Out	Run Time	Extra Dry	Total
		am pm	am pm	am pm	hrs	hrs	hrs
Start Date:		Customize Temp	Time	Check Time:	am pm	am pm	am pm
End Date:		Freeze / Dry		mTorr:			Subtract Dry from Wet for Water Loss
Tray Contents Description:	Examples: Raw, Cooked, Thickness, Liquid, Spread		Pre-Frozen	Wet grams	Check 1 grams	Check 2 grams	Dry grams
1			Y / N				
2			Y / N				
3			Y / N				
4			Y / N				
Notes			Chamber Cleaned: Y / N	Oil Changed: Y / N	Maint. Needed: Y / N		

M   FREEZE-DRYER BATCH LOGS   PAGE#

Keep track of how the foods process in your freeze-dryer.

Batch #		Start Cooling	Trays In	Trays Out	Run Time	Extra Dry	Total
		am pm	am pm	am pm	hrs	hrs	hrs
Start Date:		Customize	Temp	Time	Check Time:	am pm	am pm	am pm	
End Date:		Freeze							Subtract Dry from Wet for Water Loss
		Dry			mTorr:				
Tray Contents Description:	Examples: Raw, Cooked, Thickness, Liquid, Spread		Pre-Frozen	Wet grams	Check 1 grams	Check 2 grams	Dry grams	
1			Y / N					
2			Y / N					
3			Y / N					
4			Y / N					
Notes				Chamber Cleaned: Y / N	Oil Changed: Y / N	Maint. Needed: Y / N	

Batch #		Start Cooling	Trays In	Trays Out	Run Time	Extra Dry	Total
		am pm	am pm	am pm	hrs	hrs	hrs
Start Date:		Customize	Temp	Time	Check Time:	am pm	am pm	am pm	
End Date:		Freeze							Subtract Dry from Wet for Water Loss
		Dry			mTorr:				
Tray Contents Description:	Examples: Raw, Cooked, Thickness, Liquid, Spread		Pre-Frozen	Wet grams	Check 1 grams	Check 2 grams	Dry grams	
1			Y / N					
2			Y / N					
3			Y / N					
4			Y / N					
Notes				Chamber Cleaned: Y / N	Oil Changed: Y / N	Maint. Needed: Y / N	

Batch #		Start Cooling	Trays In	Trays Out	Run Time	Extra Dry	Total
		am pm	am pm	am pm	hrs	hrs	hrs
Start Date:		Customize	Temp	Time	Check Time:	am pm	am pm	am pm	
End Date:		Freeze							Subtract Dry from Wet for Water Loss
		Dry			mTorr:				
Tray Contents Description:	Examples: Raw, Cooked, Thickness, Liquid, Spread		Pre-Frozen	Wet grams	Check 1 grams	Check 2 grams	Dry grams	
1			Y / N					
2			Y / N					
3			Y / N					
4			Y / N					
Notes				Chamber Cleaned: Y / N	Oil Changed: Y / N	Maint. Needed: Y / N	

M   FREEZE-DRYER BATCH LOGS

Keep track of how the foods process in your freeze-dryer.

Batch #		Start Cooling	Trays In	Trays Out	Run Time	Extra Dry	Total
		am pm	am pm	am pm	hrs	hrs	hrs
Start Date:		Customize Temp Time		Check Time:	am pm	am pm	am pm
End Date:		Freeze ___ Dry ___		mTorr:			Subtract Dry from Wet for Water Loss
Tray Contents Description:	Examples: Raw, Cooked, Thickness, Liquid, Spread		Pre-Frozen	Wet grams	Check 1 grams	Check 2 grams	Dry grams	
1			Y / N					
2			Y / N					
3			Y / N					
4			Y / N					
Notes				Chamber Cleaned: Y / N	Oil Changed: Y / N	Maint. Needed: Y / N	

Batch #		Start Cooling	Trays In	Trays Out	Run Time	Extra Dry	Total
		am pm	am pm	am pm	hrs	hrs	hrs
Start Date:		Customize Temp Time		Check Time:	am pm	am pm	am pm
End Date:		Freeze ___ Dry ___		mTorr:			Subtract Dry from Wet for Water Loss
Tray Contents Description:	Examples: Raw, Cooked, Thickness, Liquid, Spread		Pre-Frozen	Wet grams	Check 1 grams	Check 2 grams	Dry grams	
1			Y / N					
2			Y / N					
3			Y / N					
4			Y / N					
Notes				Chamber Cleaned: Y / N	Oil Changed: Y / N	Maint. Needed: Y / N	

Batch #		Start Cooling	Trays In	Trays Out	Run Time	Extra Dry	Total
		am pm	am pm	am pm	hrs	hrs	hrs
Start Date:		Customize Temp Time		Check Time:	am pm	am pm	am pm
End Date:		Freeze ___ Dry ___		mTorr:			Subtract Dry from Wet for Water Loss
Tray Contents Description:	Examples: Raw, Cooked, Thickness, Liquid, Spread		Pre-Frozen	Wet grams	Check 1 grams	Check 2 grams	Dry grams	
1			Y / N					
2			Y / N					
3			Y / N					
4			Y / N					
Notes				Chamber Cleaned: Y / N	Oil Changed: Y / N	Maint. Needed: Y / N	

M FREEZE-DRYER BATCH LOGS

Keep track of how the foods process in your freeze-dryer.

Batch #		Start Cooling	Trays In	Trays Out	Run Time	Extra Dry	Total
		am pm	am pm	am pm	hrs	hrs	hrs
Start Date:		Customize	Temp	Time	Check Time:	am pm	am pm	am pm	
End Date:		Freeze							Subtract Dry from Wet for Water Loss
		Dry			mTorr:				
Tray Contents Description:	Examples: Raw, Cooked, Thickness, Liquid, Spread	Pre-Frozen	Wet grams	Check 1 grams	Check 2 grams	Dry grams	
1		Y / N					
2		Y / N					
3		Y / N					
4		Y / N					
Notes			Chamber Cleaned: Y / N	Oil Changed: Y / N	Maint. Needed: Y / N		

Batch #		Start Cooling	Trays In	Trays Out	Run Time	Extra Dry	Total
		am pm	am pm	am pm	hrs	hrs	hrs
Start Date:		Customize	Temp	Time	Check Time:	am pm	am pm	am pm	
End Date:		Freeze							Subtract Dry from Wet for Water Loss
		Dry			mTorr:				
Tray Contents Description:	Examples: Raw, Cooked, Thickness, Liquid, Spread	Pre-Frozen	Wet grams	Check 1 grams	Check 2 grams	Dry grams	
1		Y / N					
2		Y / N					
3		Y / N					
4		Y / N					
Notes			Chamber Cleaned: Y / N	Oil Changed: Y / N	Maint. Needed: Y / N		

Batch #		Start Cooling	Trays In	Trays Out	Run Time	Extra Dry	Total
		am pm	am pm	am pm	hrs	hrs	hrs
Start Date:		Customize	Temp	Time	Check Time:	am pm	am pm	am pm	
End Date:		Freeze							Subtract Dry from Wet for Water Loss
		Dry			mTorr:				
Tray Contents Description:	Examples: Raw, Cooked, Thickness, Liquid, Spread	Pre-Frozen	Wet grams	Check 1 grams	Check 2 grams	Dry grams	
1		Y / N					
2		Y / N					
3		Y / N					
4		Y / N					
Notes			Chamber Cleaned: Y / N	Oil Changed: Y / N	Maint. Needed: Y / N		

Keep track of how the foods process in your freeze-dryer.

Batch #		Start Cooling	Trays In	Trays Out	Run Time	Extra Dry	Total
		am pm	am pm	am pm	hrs	hrs	hrs
Start Date:		Customize Temp	Time	Check Time:	am pm	am pm	am pm
End Date:		Freeze					Subtract Dry from Wet for Water Loss
		Dry		mTorr:			
Tray Contents Description:	Examples: Raw, Cooked, Thickness, Liquid, Spread	Pre-Frozen	Wet grams	Check 1 grams	Check 2 grams	Dry grams	
1		Y / N					
2		Y / N					
3		Y / N					
4		Y / N					
Notes			Chamber Cleaned: Y / N	Oil Changed: Y / N	Maint. Needed: Y / N		

Batch #		Start Cooling	Trays In	Trays Out	Run Time	Extra Dry	Total
		am pm	am pm	am pm	hrs	hrs	hrs
Start Date:		Customize Temp	Time	Check Time:	am pm	am pm	am pm
End Date:		Freeze					Subtract Dry from Wet for Water Loss
		Dry		mTorr:			
Tray Contents Description:	Examples: Raw, Cooked, Thickness, Liquid, Spread	Pre-Frozen	Wet grams	Check 1 grams	Check 2 grams	Dry grams	
1		Y / N					
2		Y / N					
3		Y / N					
4		Y / N					
Notes			Chamber Cleaned: Y / N	Oil Changed: Y / N	Maint. Needed: Y / N		

Batch #		Start Cooling	Trays In	Trays Out	Run Time	Extra Dry	Total
		am pm	am pm	am pm	hrs	hrs	hrs
Start Date:		Customize Temp	Time	Check Time:	am pm	am pm	am pm
End Date:		Freeze					Subtract Dry from Wet for Water Loss
		Dry		mTorr:			
Tray Contents Description:	Examples: Raw, Cooked, Thickness, Liquid, Spread	Pre-Frozen	Wet grams	Check 1 grams	Check 2 grams	Dry grams	
1		Y / N					
2		Y / N					
3		Y / N					
4		Y / N					
Notes			Chamber Cleaned: Y / N	Oil Changed: Y / N	Maint. Needed: Y / N		

Keep track of how the foods process in your freeze-dryer.

Batch #		Start Cooling	Trays In	Trays Out	Run Time	Extra Dry	Total
		am pm	am pm	am pm	hrs	hrs	hrs
Start Date:		Customize Temp	Time	Check Time:	am pm	am pm	am pm
End Date:		Freeze					Subtract Dry from Wet for Water Loss
		Dry		mTorr:			
Tray Contents Description:	Examples: Raw, Cooked, Thickness, Liquid, Spread	Pre-Frozen	Wet grams	Check 1 grams	Check 2 grams	Dry grams	
1		Y / N					
2		Y / N					
3		Y / N					
4		Y / N					
Notes			Chamber Cleaned: Y / N	Oil Changed: Y / N	Maint. Needed: Y / N		

Batch #		Start Cooling	Trays In	Trays Out	Run Time	Extra Dry	Total
		am pm	am pm	am pm	hrs	hrs	hrs
Start Date:		Customize Temp	Time	Check Time:	am pm	am pm	am pm
End Date:		Freeze					Subtract Dry from Wet for Water Loss
		Dry		mTorr:			
Tray Contents Description:	Examples: Raw, Cooked, Thickness, Liquid, Spread	Pre-Frozen	Wet grams	Check 1 grams	Check 2 grams	Dry grams	
1		Y / N					
2		Y / N					
3		Y / N					
4		Y / N					
Notes			Chamber Cleaned: Y / N	Oil Changed: Y / N	Maint. Needed: Y / N		

Batch #		Start Cooling	Trays In	Trays Out	Run Time	Extra Dry	Total
		am pm	am pm	am pm	hrs	hrs	hrs
Start Date:		Customize Temp	Time	Check Time:	am pm	am pm	am pm
End Date:		Freeze					Subtract Dry from Wet for Water Loss
		Dry		mTorr:			
Tray Contents Description:	Examples: Raw, Cooked, Thickness, Liquid, Spread	Pre-Frozen	Wet grams	Check 1 grams	Check 2 grams	Dry grams	
1		Y / N					
2		Y / N					
3		Y / N					
4		Y / N					
Notes			Chamber Cleaned: Y / N	Oil Changed: Y / N	Maint. Needed: Y / N		

M FREEZE-DRYER BATCH LOGS   PAGE#

Keep track of how the foods process in your freeze-dryer.

Batch #		Start Cooling	Trays In	Trays Out	Run Time	Extra Dry	Total
		am pm	am pm	am pm	hrs	hrs	hrs
Start Date:		Customize Temp	Time	Check Time:	am pm	am pm	am pm
End Date:		Freeze					
		Dry		mTorr:			Subtract Dry from Wet for Water Loss
Tray Contents Description:	Examples: Raw, Cooked, Thickness, Liquid, Spread		Pre-Frozen	Wet grams	Check 1 grams	Check 2 grams	Dry grams	
1			Y / N					
2			Y / N					
3			Y / N					
4			Y / N					
Notes				Chamber Cleaned: Y / N	Oil Changed: Y / N	Maint. Needed: Y / N	

Batch #		Start Cooling	Trays In	Trays Out	Run Time	Extra Dry	Total
		am pm	am pm	am pm	hrs	hrs	hrs
Start Date:		Customize Temp	Time	Check Time:	am pm	am pm	am pm
End Date:		Freeze					
		Dry		mTorr:			Subtract Dry from Wet for Water Loss
Tray Contents Description:	Examples: Raw, Cooked, Thickness, Liquid, Spread		Pre-Frozen	Wet grams	Check 1 grams	Check 2 grams	Dry grams	
1			Y / N					
2			Y / N					
3			Y / N					
4			Y / N					
Notes				Chamber Cleaned: Y / N	Oil Changed: Y / N	Maint. Needed: Y / N	

Batch #		Start Cooling	Trays In	Trays Out	Run Time	Extra Dry	Total
		am pm	am pm	am pm	hrs	hrs	hrs
Start Date:		Customize Temp	Time	Check Time:	am pm	am pm	am pm
End Date:		Freeze					
		Dry		mTorr:			Subtract Dry from Wet for Water Loss
Tray Contents Description:	Examples: Raw, Cooked, Thickness, Liquid, Spread		Pre-Frozen	Wet grams	Check 1 grams	Check 2 grams	Dry grams	
1			Y / N					
2			Y / N					
3			Y / N					
4			Y / N					
Notes				Chamber Cleaned: Y / N	Oil Changed: Y / N	Maint. Needed: Y / N	

Keep track of how the foods process in your freeze-dryer.

Batch #		Start Cooling	Trays In	Trays Out	Run Time	Extra Dry	Total
		am pm	am pm	am pm	hrs	hrs	hrs
Start Date:		Customize	Temp	Time	Check Time:	am pm	am pm	am pm	
End Date:		Freeze / Dry			mTorr:				Subtract Dry from Wet for Water Loss
Tray Contents Description:	Examples: Raw, Cooked, Thickness, Liquid, Spread		Pre-Frozen	Wet grams	Check 1 grams	Check 2 grams	Dry grams	
1			Y / N					
2			Y / N					
3			Y / N					
4			Y / N					
Notes				Chamber Cleaned: Y / N	Oil Changed: Y / N	Maint. Needed: Y / N	

Batch #		Start Cooling	Trays In	Trays Out	Run Time	Extra Dry	Total
		am pm	am pm	am pm	hrs	hrs	hrs
Start Date:		Customize	Temp	Time	Check Time:	am pm	am pm	am pm	
End Date:		Freeze / Dry			mTorr:				Subtract Dry from Wet for Water Loss
Tray Contents Description:	Examples: Raw, Cooked, Thickness, Liquid, Spread		Pre-Frozen	Wet grams	Check 1 grams	Check 2 grams	Dry grams	
1			Y / N					
2			Y / N					
3			Y / N					
4			Y / N					
Notes				Chamber Cleaned: Y / N	Oil Changed: Y / N	Maint. Needed: Y / N	

Batch #		Start Cooling	Trays In	Trays Out	Run Time	Extra Dry	Total
		am pm	am pm	am pm	hrs	hrs	hrs
Start Date:		Customize	Temp	Time	Check Time:	am pm	am pm	am pm	
End Date:		Freeze / Dry			mTorr:				Subtract Dry from Wet for Water Loss
Tray Contents Description:	Examples: Raw, Cooked, Thickness, Liquid, Spread		Pre-Frozen	Wet grams	Check 1 grams	Check 2 grams	Dry grams	
1			Y / N					
2			Y / N					
3			Y / N					
4			Y / N					
Notes				Chamber Cleaned: Y / N	Oil Changed: Y / N	Maint. Needed: Y / N	

Keep track of how the foods process in your freeze-dryer.

Batch #		Start Cooling	Trays In	Trays Out	Run Time	Extra Dry	Total
		am pm	am pm	am pm	hrs	hrs	hrs
Start Date:		Customize Temp	Time	Check Time:	am pm	am pm	am pm
End Date:		Freeze					Subtract Dry from Wet for Water Loss
		Dry		mTorr:			
Tray Contents Description:	Examples: Raw, Cooked, Thickness, Liquid, Spread	Pre-Frozen	Wet grams	Check 1 grams	Check 2 grams	Dry grams	
1		Y / N					
2		Y / N					
3		Y / N					
4		Y / N					
Notes			Chamber Cleaned: Y / N	Oil Changed: Y / N	Maint. Needed: Y / N		

Batch #		Start Cooling	Trays In	Trays Out	Run Time	Extra Dry	Total
		am pm	am pm	am pm	hrs	hrs	hrs
Start Date:		Customize Temp	Time	Check Time:	am pm	am pm	am pm
End Date:		Freeze					Subtract Dry from Wet for Water Loss
		Dry		mTorr:			
Tray Contents Description:	Examples: Raw, Cooked, Thickness, Liquid, Spread	Pre-Frozen	Wet grams	Check 1 grams	Check 2 grams	Dry grams	
1		Y / N					
2		Y / N					
3		Y / N					
4		Y / N					
Notes			Chamber Cleaned: Y / N	Oil Changed: Y / N	Maint. Needed: Y / N		

Batch #		Start Cooling	Trays In	Trays Out	Run Time	Extra Dry	Total
		am pm	am pm	am pm	hrs	hrs	hrs
Start Date:		Customize Temp	Time	Check Time:	am pm	am pm	am pm
End Date:		Freeze					Subtract Dry from Wet for Water Loss
		Dry		mTorr:			
Tray Contents Description:	Examples: Raw, Cooked, Thickness, Liquid, Spread	Pre-Frozen	Wet grams	Check 1 grams	Check 2 grams	Dry grams	
1		Y / N					
2		Y / N					
3		Y / N					
4		Y / N					
Notes			Chamber Cleaned: Y / N	Oil Changed: Y / N	Maint. Needed: Y / N		

Keep track of how the foods process in your freeze-dryer.

Batch #		Start Cooling	Trays In	Trays Out	Run Time		Extra Dry		Total	
		am pm	am pm	am pm	hrs		hrs		hrs	
Start Date:		Customize	Temp	Time	Check Time:	am pm		am pm	am pm	Subtract Dry from Wet for Water Loss
End Date:		Freeze Dry			mTorr:					
Tray Contents Description:	Examples: Raw, Cooked, Thickness, Liquid, Spread		Pre-Frozen	Wet grams	Check 1 grams		Check 2 grams		Dry grams	
1			Y / N							
2			Y / N							
3			Y / N							
4			Y / N							
Notes				Chamber Cleaned: Y / N	Oil Changed: Y / N		Maint. Needed: Y / N			

Batch #		Start Cooling	Trays In	Trays Out	Run Time		Extra Dry		Total	
		am pm	am pm	am pm	hrs		hrs		hrs	
Start Date:		Customize	Temp	Time	Check Time:	am pm		am pm	am pm	Subtract Dry from Wet for Water Loss
End Date:		Freeze Dry			mTorr:					
Tray Contents Description:	Examples: Raw, Cooked, Thickness, Liquid, Spread		Pre-Frozen	Wet grams	Check 1 grams		Check 2 grams		Dry grams	
1			Y / N							
2			Y / N							
3			Y / N							
4			Y / N							
Notes				Chamber Cleaned: Y / N	Oil Changed: Y / N		Maint. Needed: Y / N			

Batch #		Start Cooling	Trays In	Trays Out	Run Time		Extra Dry		Total	
		am pm	am pm	am pm	hrs		hrs		hrs	
Start Date:		Customize	Temp	Time	Check Time:	am pm		am pm	am pm	Subtract Dry from Wet for Water Loss
End Date:		Freeze Dry			mTorr:					
Tray Contents Description:	Examples: Raw, Cooked, Thickness, Liquid, Spread		Pre-Frozen	Wet grams	Check 1 grams		Check 2 grams		Dry grams	
1			Y / N							
2			Y / N							
3			Y / N							
4			Y / N							
Notes				Chamber Cleaned: Y / N	Oil Changed: Y / N		Maint. Needed: Y / N			

M FREEZE-DRYER BATCH LOGS

Keep track of how the foods process in your freeze-dryer.

Batch #		Start Cooling	Trays In	Trays Out	Run Time	Extra Dry	Total
		am pm	am pm	am pm	hrs	hrs	hrs
Start Date:		Customize	Temp	Time	Check Time:	am pm	am pm	am pm	
End Date:		Freeze Dry			mTorr:				Subtract Dry from Wet for Water Loss
Tray Contents Description:	Examples: Raw, Cooked, Thickness, Liquid, Spread		Pre-Frozen	Wet grams	Check 1 grams	Check 2 grams	Dry grams	
1			Y / N					
2			Y / N					
3			Y / N					
4			Y / N					
Notes			Chamber Cleaned: Y / N	Oil Changed: Y / N	Maint. Needed: Y / N		

Batch #		Start Cooling	Trays In	Trays Out	Run Time	Extra Dry	Total
		am pm	am pm	am pm	hrs	hrs	hrs
Start Date:		Customize	Temp	Time	Check Time:	am pm	am pm	am pm	
End Date:		Freeze Dry			mTorr:				Subtract Dry from Wet for Water Loss
Tray Contents Description:	Examples: Raw, Cooked, Thickness, Liquid, Spread		Pre-Frozen	Wet grams	Check 1 grams	Check 2 grams	Dry grams	
1			Y / N					
2			Y / N					
3			Y / N					
4			Y / N					
Notes			Chamber Cleaned: Y / N	Oil Changed: Y / N	Maint. Needed: Y / N		

Batch #		Start Cooling	Trays In	Trays Out	Run Time	Extra Dry	Total
		am pm	am pm	am pm	hrs	hrs	hrs
Start Date:		Customize	Temp	Time	Check Time:	am pm	am pm	am pm	
End Date:		Freeze Dry			mTorr:				Subtract Dry from Wet for Water Loss
Tray Contents Description:	Examples: Raw, Cooked, Thickness, Liquid, Spread		Pre-Frozen	Wet grams	Check 1 grams	Check 2 grams	Dry grams	
1			Y / N					
2			Y / N					
3			Y / N					
4			Y / N					
Notes			Chamber Cleaned: Y / N	Oil Changed: Y / N	Maint. Needed: Y / N		

GETTING STARTED CHECKLIST

Approve & Inspect Items in Your Order

- ☐ Inspect for Damage (HR: 801-386-8960)
- ☐ Harvest Right Freeze-dryer
- ☐ Shelving unit (inside the appliance)
- ☐ 6' power cord (black)
- ☐ Drain line tubing (clear)
- ☐ Vacuum pump
- ☐ Vacuum hose (black)
- ☐ Vacuum pump oil (unless oil-free)
- ☐ Oil filter (unless oil-free)
- ☐ Impulse sealer
- ☐ Stainless steel trays (S: 3, M: 4, L: 5, XL: 6)
- ☐ Package of Mylar bags
- ☐ Package of oxygen absorbers (OA)
- ☐ Harvest Right owner's manual
- ☐ Harvest Right Guide to Freeze-drying
- ☐ Additional Accessories

Positioning your Machine

- ☐ Carefully Move into position
- ☐ Environment is Clean & Dry
- ☐ Room Temperature is Cool (45°F - 75°F)
- ☐ Adequate Ventilation on both sides
- ☐ Table, Cart, or Countertop
- ☐ Surface is stable and level

Tasks while you Wait

- ☐ Read the Harvest Right Owner's Manual.
- ☐ Open the door and ensure the shelving unit is connected and positioned correctly.
- ☐ Inspect the rubber gasket & acrylic door and wipe with warm water and a cotton cloth.
- ☐ Attach the drain hose to the fitting on the side of the appliance.
- ☐ Allow the vinyl hose to fall into a 5-gallon bucket while hanging loosely.
- ☐ Add the ⅜" Y fittings to your tubing by cutting the line & pushing the ends onto the fitting.
- ☐ Attach the power cord, but do not plug it in until the 24 hours have passed.
- ☐ Position the pump by placing it on the right side or below the freeze-dryer. (oil-free above)
- ☐ Add the included oil to your pump up to just above the centerline.
- ☐ Attach vacuum hose to fitting on right side & attach the other end to the pump.
- ☐ Plug the pump into the receptacle on the back of the freeze-dryer.
- ☐ Flip the vacuum pump switch to the ON position. (It won't turn on.)
- ☐ Place fans to blow directly on the left side of the appliance.
- ☐ Find locations for your equipment: impulse sealer, food funnel, FoodSaver®, etc.
- ☐ Find a good storage place for your packaging materials: Mylar bags and oxygen absorbers.
- ☐ Store your accessories: silicone mats, molds, parchment, dividers, corner stackers, etc.

After the 24 hours

- ☐ Plug freeze-dryer into prepared outlet
- ☐ Close drain valve on side of freeze-dryer
- ☐ Close door in two turns & check seal
- ☐ Flip power switch to ON position
- ☐ Test the Freeze function (40 min)
- ☐ Test the Vacuum function (30 min)
- ☐ Set up the Interface (10 min)
- ☐ Complete the Bread Run (24 hours)

FREEZE-DRYING STEPS

Putting Food IN to your Freeze-Dryer

1. Prepare food to ½" - ¾" thickness or into pieces.
2. Pre-freeze for 24-48 hrs. This improves appliance efficiency & avoids messes.
3. Check the Oil in the Pump. It should be clear and between half-full and max.
4. Plug in the freeze-dryer, flip the Switch on, seat the Gasket, close the Door, check the Seal, and fully latch the Handle.
5. On the Customize Screen, set any changes in Temperature & Time.
6. Press Start to begin pre-cooling the chamber (minimum 15-90 min.)
7. Point a fan on the left side of the freeze-dryer.
8. Wait for the Prompt (after 15+ min,) and close the Drain Valve.
9. Weigh the trays. Put the food trays in, close the Door, check the Seal, and fully latch the Handle.
10. Press Continue and wait for 24-60+ hours. Start prepping the next batch.

Taking Food OUT of your Freeze-Dryer

1. When the three phases are complete Extra Dry Time starts. You can cancel anytime to check the food. Set Extra Dry Time to 24 hours. You can't overdry.
2. Ensure the drain hose is in an empty bucket, press Cancel, slowly open the Drain Valve & wait 5 min for pressure to release.
3. Open the Door, remove the food, & check for cold or soft spots. Weigh each tray.
4. Put trays back in. Set More Dry Time to 4+ hours and check the weight in 2 hours. Repeat as needed. When weight doesn't change it is fully dry & can be packaged.
5. Remove the food from the trays and put them immediately into proper storage. (7-mil Mylar bag heat sealed with OA or canning jar vacuum sealed with an OA.)
6. Add an Oxygen Absorber (OA). 100cc/quart, 300cc/gallon.
7. Remove excess oxygen. Seal the Mylar bag or canning jar.
8. Defrost the Chamber by opening the door (or select Defrost.)
9. Clean the freeze-dryer components with a soft cloth and warm water. Sterilize with isopropyl alcohol or Everclear.
10. Aim a fan directly in the chamber to help get it dry. Then start the next batch.

FREEZE-DRYER SCREENS

Harvest Right™ System Configuration

Appliance Log, Serial Number, Hours Running,
Number of Batches, Temperature °F to °C,
Set Time button, and Pump button.

Set Time: Date, Time, Alarm
Pump: Select Type, Reset Hours

Leaf: Functional Testing

Freeze, Vacuum, Heater, and Aux Relay

Customize: Freeze & Dry

Temperatures & Times

Customize Defaults:
Initial freeze: -10°F
Extra Freeze Time: 0:00
Dry Mode Normal
Dry Temp.: 125°F
Extra Dry Time: 2:00
  (Recommended 12:00 - 24:00)

Start

Begins the process by Cooling the chamber

System Name

Your Choice of a Name

REHYDRATION INFORMATION

Rehydration is not always necessary.

If you want a crunchy snack, just eat it right out of the bag or jar.

If you are making soup add the freeze-dried food to the pot and add water as needed.

Fruits & vegetables best used dry can be blended into a powder & added to soups, sauces, or smoothies.

Some foods require much less water to rehydrate. Start with less (HALF) and add more slowly.

Rehydration General Rule of Thumb:

+

1 cup Freeze-dried Food

½ - 1 cup Water* (start with ½ cup)

*Add a small amount of water gradually, stir or turn items, and add the rest as needed.

Meals 5-20+ min	Add hot water, stir, and allow it to sit. Or, break it up in an oven-safe dish, add hot water, cover, and bake in the oven like a casserole.
Cooked Meats 5-60 min	Place the food in a dish and add just enough hot water to cover. Too much water can turn cooked meats into mush.
Fruits & Vegetables 1-10 min	Lay out food on a tray & spritz lightly with cold water. Flip or stir to get the other side. Allow it to soak in & then spritz more as needed.
Raw Meats 30 min - 3+ hrs	Place the raw meat in a dish, add cold water or broth, and place in the fridge overnight. Pat dry with paper towel and thoroughly cook.
Eggs 2-5 min	Add 2 Tablespoons egg powder to 2 Tablespoons cold water. Stir and allow it to sit a few minutes. Use as you would a raw egg.
Powders 2-5 min	Add small amounts of cold water and stir. It is typically about 50:50 water to powder, regardless of what kind of powder.
Cheeses 5-15 min	Wrap cheese slices in moist paper towels & allow to sit. Spritz shredded cheese with cold water. Other cheeses are best dry or added to recipes.
Desserts 5-10 min	Place the treat & a moist paper towel inside a Ziploc bag & allow to sit. Alternatively, wrap the treat in a moist paper towel. Or just eat crunchy!

*Note: Some foods will take considerably longer to rehydrate than others in the same category.

Determine Water Needed for Portion Rehydration

Portion weight (in grams)		Total Water Removed (g)	Multiply By Chosen Unit	Total Water Needed
Prior to FD	After FD			
_____ g	_____ g	_____ g	x 0.00423 cup	_____ c
_____ g	_____ g	_____ g	x 0.06667 Tbs	_____ T
_____ g	_____ g	_____ g	x 0.23471 tsp	_____ t
_____ g	_____ g	_____ g	x 0.03527 oz	_____ oz

*Note: 1 gram of water = 0.00423 cups = 0.0667 Tablespoons = 0.2347 teaspoons = 0.03527 ounces

CONVERSIONS

Use these handy conversions to make life in the kitchen a little easier.

1 CUP =
16 tablespoons,
8 ounces
240 ml

1/2 CUP =
8 tablespoons
120 ml

1 PINT =
2 cups,
16 ounces
480 ml

1 GALLON =
4 quarts,
8 pints,
16 cups,
128 ounces
3.8 liters

1 QUART =
2 pints,
4 cups,
32 ounces,
950 ml

1 teaspoon = 5 ml
1 tablespoon = 3 teaspoons = 15 ml
2 tablespoons = 1 ounce = 30 ml
4 tablespoons = 1/4 cup = 60 ml
5 tablespoons + 1 teaspoon = 80 ml

oz	grams	lbs
1/2	14	
3/4	21	
1	28	
2	57	1/8
3	85	
4	113	1/4
5	142	
6	170	
7	198	
8	227	1/2
9	255	
10	284	
11	312	
12	340	3/4
13	369	
14	397	
15	425	
16	454	1
24	680	1.5
32	907	2
40	1134	2.5
48	1361	3
56	1588	3.5
64	1814	4
72	2041	4.5
80	2268	5

FOODS YOU CANNOT FREEZE-DRY

Oily or Fatty Foods and Sugary foods do not freeze-dry well.
Small amounts within prepared recipes generally work out fine.

Any meals or foods that contain oils should be used within
1-5 years due to the nature of fats, which go rancid over time.

FREEZE-DRYER NO'S

High Fat:

- Oils
- Butter
- Mayonnaise
- Pure Chocolate
- Nuts
- Nut Butters
- Nutella
- Peanut Butter

High Sugar:

- Honey
- Syrup
- Soda
- Jam
- Jelly
- Preserves

Treats:

- Twizzlers
- Licorice
- Oreos
- Candy Canes
- Swedish Fish
- Fruit Snacks
- Gum Drops
- Cinnamon Disks

Other:

- Bones
- Alcohol
- Vinegar
- Water (lol!)

GREAT FOODS TO FREEZE-DRY

Fruits

- Apples
- Apricots
- Avocado
- Bananas
- Blackberries
- Blueberries
- Cantaloupe
- Cherries
- Coconut
- Cranberry
- Currants
- Dewberries
- Elderberries
- Figs
- Goji Berries
- Gooseberries
- Grapefruit
- Grapes
- Ground cherries
- Honeydew

- Kiwifruit
- Lemons
- Limes
- Mandarins
- Mangos
- Mulberries
- Nectarines
- Oranges
- Passion Fruit
- Peaches
- Pears
- Pineapple
- Plums
- Pomegranate
- Raspberries
- Rhubarb
- Star Fruits
- Strawberries
- Tangerines
- Watermelon

Snacks

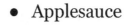

- Applesauce
- Breads
- Croutons
- Diluted BBQ Sauce
- Diluted Ketchup
- Diluted Mustard
- French Onion Dip
- Guacamole

- Nacho Cheese
- Pickles
- Pizza
- Ranch Dip
- Refried Beans
- Salsa
- Sourdough Starter
- Sweet Breads

GREAT FOODS TO FREEZE-DRY

Vegetables

- Asparagus
- Beets
- Bok Choy
- Broad Beans
- Broccoli
- Brussel Sprouts
- Cabbage
- Carrots
- Cauliflower
- Celery
- Corn
- Cucumber
- Eggplant
- Garlic
- Green beans
- Greens
- Kale
- Kohlrabi
- Leeks
- Lettuce
- Mushrooms
- Okra

- Onions
- Parsnips
- Peas, Green
- Peas, Snap
- Peppers, Hot
- Peppers, Sweet
- Potatoes
- Pumpkins
- Radish
- Rutabaga
- Scallions
- Spinach
- Squash, Butternut
- Squash, Spaghetti
- Squash, Yellow
- Squash, Zucchini
- Sweet potatoes
- Swiss chard
- Tomatillos
- Tomatoes
- Turnips
- Yams

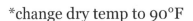

*change dry temp to 90°F

Dairy

- Buttermilk
- Cheese Curds
- Condensed Milk
- Cottage Cheese
- Cow Milk
- Cream Cheese
- Custard
- Goat Milk

- Hard Cheeses
- Heavy Cream
- Ice Cream
- Kefir*
- Soft Cheeses
- Sour Cream
- Whipped Cream
- Yogurt*

GREAT FOODS TO FREEZE-DRY

Meats

Beef - Lean

- Cubed Steak
- Deli Meat
- Ground
- Filets
- Kabobs
- Meatballs
- Patties
- Roast
- Shredded
- Strips
- Steaks
- Stew Meats

Pork - Lean

- Bacon
- Chops
- Ham
- Loin
- Roast
- Shredded

Poultry

- Chopped
- Ground
- Roasted
- Shredded
- Sliced
- Turkey Bacon
- Game Fowl

Other

Bison, Boar, Elk, Deer, Goat, Rabbit, Sheep

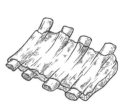

Seafood

Freshwater

- Bass
- Bluegill
- Carp
- Catfish
- Perch
- Tilapia
- Trout
- Walleye

Saltwater

- Cod
- Flounder
- Redfish
- Snapper
- Salmon
- Sheepshead
- Swordfish
- Tuna

Shellfish

- Clam
- Crab
- Lobster
- Mussel
- Octopus
- Oyster
- Scallop
- Shrimp

GREAT FOODS TO FREEZE-DRY

Meals

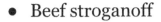

- Beef stroganoff
- Breakfast Skillet
- Casseroles
- Cheese steak
- Chicken parmesan
- Chili
- Chow mein
- Creole
- Enchiladas
- Fajitas
- Goulash
- Gumbo
- Hamburger patties
- Hash browns
- Jambalaya
- Lasagna
- Macaroni & Cheese
- Mashed potatoes
- Meatballs
- Meat Loaf
- Oatmeal
- Pasta
- Pizza Casserole
- Roast Turkey Dinner
- Roast Beef Dinner
- Soups
- Spaghetti
- Stews
- Tacos
- Tuna Salad

Drinks

- Bone Broth
- Broth
- Carrot Juice
- Coconut Water
- Coffee
- Cow Milk
- Eggnog
- Fruit Juices
- Fruit Smoothies
- Goat Milk
- Grapefruit Juice
- Green Machine
- Greens Juices
- Hot Cocoa
- Lemon Juice
- Lime Juice
- Milkshakes
- Oat Milk
- Orange Juice
- Pineapple Juice
- Protein Shakes
- Prune Juice
- Rice Milks
- Smoothies
- Supplements
- Tomato Juice
- V8 & Fusions
- Vegetable Juices

GREAT FOODS TO FREEZE-DRY

Legumes & Grains

- Chickpeas
- Beans
- Lentils
- Peas
- Soybeans
- Sprouts
- Barley
- Oats
- Quinoa
- Rice
- Rye
- Wheat
- Bread
- Cake
- Cookies
- Crackers
- Granola
- Pasta

Desserts

- Cake
- Cheesecake
- Cookies
- Ice Cream
- Ice Cream Sandwiches
- Jell-O
- Lemon Bars
- Marshmallows
- Mousse
- Pie
- Pudding
- Shortcake
- Tarts
- Twinkies

*use Candy mode

Candies*

Use Whole
- Candy Corn
- Caramel Apple Pops
- Caramel M&M's
- Gummy Bears
- Gummy Worms
- Junior Mints
- Lemonheads
- Life Saver Gummies
- Mamba
- Peach Rings
- Skittles
- Stuffed Puffs

Cut into Pieces
- Airheads (⅓)
- Bit 'O Honey (⅓)
- Caramels (½)
- Jolly Ranchers (⅓)
- Laffy Taffy (¼)
- Milk Duds (½)
- Mini Milky Way (½)
- Salt Water Taffy (¼)
- Mini Snickers (½)
- Starburst (¼)
- Tootsie Chews (½)
- Twix (¼)

GREAT FOODS TO FREEZE-DRY

Eggs

- Cooked
- Raw (Pre-freeze Solid)
- Scrambled
- Skillets
- Casseroles
- Quiche

*change dry temp to 90°F

*Herbs**

- Basil
- Chives
- Cilantro
- Comfrey
- Dill Weed
- Fennel
- Ginger
- Ginseng
- Horseradish
- Lemon Balm
- Marjoram
- Nettle
- Oregano
- Parsley
- Peppermint
- Rosemary
- Sage
- Spearmint
- Stevia
- Tarragon
- Thyme
- Turmeric

*change dry temp to 90°F

*Edible Flowers**

- Begonia
- Borage
- Calendula
- Carnations
- Chamomile
- Chrysanthemums
- Cornflowers
- Daisies
- Dandelion
- Dianthus
- French Marigolds
- Gladioli
- Hibiscus
- Hollyhock
- Honeysuckle
- Hostas
- Lavender
- Nasturtium
- Pansies
- Roses
- Snapdragons
- Sunflowers
- Tulips
- Violas

TROUBLESHOOTING

Harvest Right™ Customer Service

The phone number is 1-801-386-8960. The website is https://harvestright.com. They have awesome customer service. They will work with you to make sure your freeze-dryer is working properly. If your machine is out of warranty they will help you get the info and parts you need so you can fix it.

The Freeze-dryer Problem Diagnosis Guide

This is the first step to getting help with your freeze-dryer when something is amiss. Here's a shortcut to the HarvestRight's website: FDHR.2MHE.COM or scan the QR Code.

On the website, go to the top right corner and click on Customer Support. Scroll down and pick a category from these options: Set Up & Basics, Vacuum Error, Refrigeration Issues, Drying Issues, Touchscreen Issues, Power Issues, and Software Versions.

From here the Diagnosis Guide will walk you through troubleshooting your particular issue. There is a lot of great help available for all kinds of issues. You can also search the customer support articles. If you don't get it worked out with the guide, then submit a ticket to get personal help. You can do that on the same page.

Facebook Groups & Pages

Join a few freeze-drying Facebook groups to connect with other people like you, check out recipe ideas and tips, and also get help troubleshooting your machine if the need arises. There are a lot of members with the information you may need and the compiled group knowledge is invaluable for getting helpful ideas quickly.

Micro-Homesteading Education's Freeze-Drying Facebook group is "Food Preservation with Freeze Drying." Connect with us! Here's the shortcut: FDFB.2MHE.COM.

MAINTENANCE LOG

Keep track of your freeze-dryer maintenance and repair expenses.

Date	Part/Service	Cost	Notes

MAINTENANCE LOG

Keep track of your freeze-dryer maintenance and repair expenses.

Date	Part/Service	Cost	Notes

MAINTENANCE LOG

Keep track of your freeze-dryer maintenance and repair expenses.

Date	Part/Service	Cost	Notes

MAINTENANCE LOG

Keep track of your freeze-dryer maintenance and repair expenses.

Date	Part/Service	Cost	Notes

MAINTENANCE LOG

Keep track of your freeze-dryer maintenance and repair expenses.

Date	Part/Service	Cost	Notes

MAINTENANCE LOG

Keep track of your freeze-dryer maintenance and repair expenses.

Date	Part/Service	Cost	Notes

MAINTENANCE LOG

Keep track of your freeze-dryer maintenance and repair expenses.

Date	Part/Service	Cost	Notes

MAINTENANCE LOG

Keep track of your freeze-dryer maintenance and repair expenses.

Date	Part/Service	Cost	Notes

MAINTENANCE LOG

Keep track of your freeze-dryer maintenance and repair expenses.

Date	Part/Service	Cost	Notes

MAINTENANCE LOG

Keep track of your freeze-dryer maintenance and repair expenses.

Date	Part/Service	Cost	Notes

NOTES

NOTES

NOTES

NOTES

NOTES

NOTES

NOTES

NOTES

NOTES

NOTES

JOIN OUR COMMUNITY

Contact Us:

Email: contact@micro-homesteading-education.com
Website: www.micro-homesteading-education.com

Facebook Groups & Pages:

www.facebook.com/microhomesteadingeducationcom
www.facebook.com/groups/foodpreservationwithfreezedrying
www.facebook.com/groups/funwithgardeningandhomesteading

Shortcut to FB Group:

Visit: FDFB.2MHE.COM

Or scan QR Code:

Printable Worksheets:

Visit: BFDPDF.2MHE.COM

Or scan QR Code:

ALSO BY

Micro-Homesteading Education

The Only Beginner Freeze Drying Book You'll Ever Need

Coming soon to Amazon:

Freeze Drying Food at Home for Backpacking Trips

Making Freeze-Dried Candy for Selling and Fun

Freeze-Dried Smoothies for Gut Health

Freeze Drying and Herbal Remedies

Made in the USA
Las Vegas, NV
18 December 2024

14627424R00079